CRAIGDARROCH CASTLE *in*

21

TREASURES

PROGRAMME.

—:—:—

1. WALTZ......................Jolly Fellows
2. LANCERS.........................Windsor
3. WALTZ.........................La Gitana
4. BARN..........................Angeline
5. WALTZ.........................Ben Bolt
6. WALTZ.........................Toreador
7. POLKA...................Black and Tan
8. WALTZ.........................Symposia
9. BARN....................Alabama Coon

EXTRAS {
  1. WALTZ ....
  2. DEUX TEMPS ....
  3. BARN ....
}

10. WALTZ......................Blue Danube
11. LANCERS........................De Gamo
12. WALTZ....................L'Estudiantina
13. WASHINGTON POST ....
14. WALTZ.........................Santiago
15. WALTZ ....Love's Dreamland
16. BARN...................Coon Wedding
17. WALTZ ....Farewell
18. WALTZ ....After the Ball

ENGAGEMENTS

—:—:—

1. ....
2. ....
3. ....
4. ....
5. ....
6. ....
7. ....
8. ....
9. ....

EXTRAS {
  1. ....
  2. ....
  3. ....
}

10. ....
11. ....
12. ....
13. ....
14. ....
15. ....
16. ....
17. ....
18. ....

CRAIGDARROCH CASTLE *in*

TREASURES

Moira Dann

TOUCHWOOD

The information in this book is true and complete to the best of the author's knowledge. All recommendations are made without guarantee on the part of the author or the publisher.

Copy edited by Meg Yamamoto
Cover and interior design by Lara Minja
Family tree on pages 20 & 21 by Sydney Barnes

CATALOGUING DATA AVAILABLE FROM LIBRARY AND ARCHIVES CANADA

ISBN 9781771513487 (print)
ISBN 9781771513494 (electronic)

TouchWood Editions acknowledges that the land on which we live and work is within the traditional territories of the Lkwungen (Esquimalt and Songhees), Malahat, Pacheedaht, Scia'new, T'Sou-ke and W̱SÁNEĆ (Pauquachin, Tsartlip, Tsawout, Tseycum) peoples.

We acknowledge the financial support of the Government of Canada through the Canada Book Fund and the Canada Council for the Arts, and of the Province of British Columbia through the British Columbia Arts Council and the Book Publishing Tax Credit.

 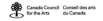 

The interior pages of this book have been printed on 100% post-consumer recycled paper, processed chlorine free, and printed with vegetable-based inks.

Printed in Canada at Friesens

25 24 23 22 21   1 2 3 4 5

Dedicated to everyone who visits Craigdarroch Castle,
and everyone interested in learning all we can
from the past so we can create a better now
and imagine a better future.

CONTENTS

ROBERT DUNSMUIR
AND JOAN DUNSMUIR

Craigdarroch Castle's Origin Story

C RAIGDARROCH CASTLE was built by the nineteenth-century coal and shipping entrepreneur Robert Dunsmuir for his wife, Joan, and their family. There's a story that Robert, while they were still in Scotland, had promised Joan he'd build her a castle in British Columbia if she accompanied him to start a new life in the New World. No matter if it's an apocryphal tale, no matter if he made that promise or not, that's what he did. A Scottish immigrant to Canada, Robert Dunsmuir made manifest the wealth he'd accumulated and the power he'd accrued in British Columbia with a symbol high on a hill in Victoria—Craigdarroch Castle.

Robert and Joan started in Canada with nothing and ended up with too much.

The couple came to Canada in 1851 from Kilmarnock in Ayrshire, Scotland. They'd been married a scant eight days before Joan gave birth to their first daughter, Elizabeth, in 1847. The pattern continued, as within ten days of arriving in North America after a six-month ocean voyage, Joan gave birth to her first son, James, in July 1851.

They started out in Fort Rupert, near the northern tip of Vancouver Island. The family moved close to Nanaimo in 1852, when Hudson's Bay Company coal interests moved that way. A few years later, Robert started working as an independent coal miner, with the blessing of the company. A number of years after that, he found a rich coal seam near Nanaimo, and he turned that into wealth, influence, and power.

Robert found partners and got into shipping coal both on Vancouver Island (to where the Royal Navy had expanded its presence) and to a developing market in San Francisco.

Next, he got into railway transport. He and some partners were able to get grants of money and land (nearly 7,700 square kilometres, a quarter of Vancouver Island) to build the Esquimalt and Nanaimo Railway, a part of Sir John A. Macdonald's dream of a national railway and a promise he'd made to British Columbians in exchange for their joining Confederation.

And then: politics. Robert was sitting as a member of the provincial legislative assembly when he moved his family to Victoria in 1883, to a house near the legislature called Fairview, on Menzies Street in the neighbourhood known as James Bay. (The Embassy Inn now sits where the Dunsmuir mansion stood.)

Building started in 1887, and sourcing the material for many of the things he wanted for this incredible nineteenth-century "bonanza castle" took time. Bonanza castles were built by men who had made fortunes in changing times; in addition to Craigdarroch, the homes of Mark Hopkins, Collis P. Huntington, Leland Stanford, and Charles Crocker (all railway "frenemies" of Robert) in San Francisco were all considered bonanza castles. Craigdarroch is one of the few still standing.

Unfortunately, Robert Dunsmuir died of renal failure in 1889, before the castle was finished. Joan and her sons continued at loggerheads over the will and the business, but the castle was finally finished. In 1890, Joan moved in with three unmarried daughters and two orphaned grandchildren.

Joan knew the power her show of wealth would exert in attracting suitable husbands for her unmarried daughters, with an additional benefit of providing the Dunsmuir family name with some old-world, titled respectability.

The lives and the legacy of the Dunsmuir family are the most in evidence at Craigdarroch Castle. And what tales the objects left behind by the castle occupants can tell!

THE FIRST STORIES are those of the Dunsmuir family, starting with Robert and Joan and their family of eight daughters and two sons. Then there are the stories of the next generation, the grandchildren. There were those who lived here with their grandmother Joan after being orphaned and those who visited (and lived) here over the years. Some of these Dunsmuir stories changed location (to James Dunsmuir's Hatley Castle, for instance), and some just faded away after Joan died and Craigdarroch went up for sale in 1909.

The next chorus of stories are those of the nurses, doctors, and "ward aides" who helped servicemen recovering from the damage done to men's bodies and minds by the Great War, when Craigdarroch was a military hospital between 1919 and 1921.

Those tales are then supplanted by those told by the babel of students' voices, male and female both, when Craigdarroch housed Victoria College. It was an outpost of Montreal's McGill University, taking up residence after the military hospital closed.

Over the years, the student body grew—but the castle didn't! The enrolment spilled over until it was deemed a health and fire hazard, and the college was moved to its new building (the former Normal School), on Lansdowne Road, in 1946.

The Victoria school board had long been the actual owner of Craigdarroch Castle (it had bought it in 1929), and after Victoria College left, the school board turned the building into its offices.

Next come the musical stories told by the instruments of the students at the Victoria Conservatory of Music. An entire generation of Victoria music students clambered up the central staircase with violins and cellos; they learned to play scales and "Für Elise" on one of thirty-odd pianos brought into the building.

In the late 1950s and into the '60s and '70s, things grew clamorous and contentious as the desire to restore the castle to its original state and operate it as a museum increased. There were a few verbal scuffles during a period when the conservatory found itself holding classes in high-traffic areas, which led to too much interruption as tour groups went through. In 1979 the conservatory moved, and the Craigdarroch Castle Historical Museum Society moved ahead with the dream to make Craigdarroch Castle a historic house museum.

And here we are, more than forty years later, with the castle's doors open to visitors, revealing its variegated history of more than a century, and telling the stories of the many people contained within the castle walls over the years.

Why I Wrote This Book

LOVE CRAIGDARROCH CASTLE; it is one of my favourite things about living in Victoria.

It is more than a majestic building atop a hill; it is a repository for so many stories and generations of echoed voices. It offers myriad opportunities for time travel and to imagine realities other than my own.

Entering the great hall (after the soles of my shoes get a good cleaning in the curved-wall porte cochère vestibule), I imagine the widow Joan Dunsmuir crossing the threshold for the first time in September 1890. I imagine her alighting from her carriage and squeezing through the tiny foyer space before emerging into the main hall and seeing the fireplace. I imagine her moving closer to read the inscription in the stone above the hearth: "Welcome ever smiles and farewell goes out sighing." I wonder if she smiles. Would she smile because it's familiar? Or does she cock her head to one side because she doesn't recognize it? (That's what I do. I later learn the quote is from Shakespeare's *Troilus and Cressida*.)

I think of Joan turning to her left to look at the first landing of the magnificent main staircase and then stepping back to crane her neck to look up at the stairs, going up four floors.

I picture her making the next move into the house, as I do: turning right and right again to enter the library. Beautiful mahogany half-wall bookcases limn the room, its focus a stained glass window over the fireplace. (How did they do that and not have the heat ruin the window? A bent-flue chimney, it turns out.) An inscription from Sir Francis Bacon says: "Reading maketh a full man."

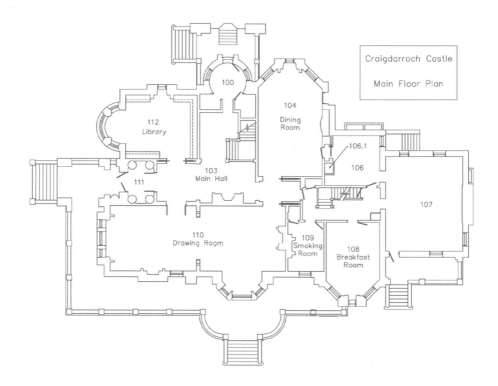

I have to stop myself from getting carried away in my imagining, as it's doubtful the room was arranged back then as it is now, with the exact same books, art, photo, and furniture choices. But I can still picture Joan looking out the three-panelled library bay window with the stained glass at the top, wishing Robert were at her side.

I leave this peaceful room and cross the hall past the Garden Entrance, the most-used entrance for a long period post-Dunsmuir, but initially meant to give nineteenth-century ladies, in their long dresses with boned bodices, and their friends (and beaux?) an easy way to get to the estate's lawns, an entree to the grounds. Out of the corner of my eye, I spot the corner radiator; it seems out of place in a building dominated by fireplaces for heating. I wonder if it was there when Joan first moved in (it was), and how the heck did they heat this massive castle anyway?

I imagine Joan going through one of two doors into the long, rectangular drawing room and casting her eye around. Much of what is there now, such as the Steinway piano, wouldn't have been there then, but the distinctive architectural features would have met her gaze: the columns at the room's midpoint, the stained glass windows, the two fireplaces, and the painted ceiling.

I have come to particularly love the drawing room. So much happened here, in the castle's many incarnations. It was a hospital ward, a classroom, and a music room. It's the location where the only extant photograph from the Dunsmuir residency was taken, featuring Joan's granddaughter Elizabeth Harvey and the daughters—Maud, Effie, and Jessie—who moved into Craigdarroch with Joan. They are reading and making music, and front and centre is the bronze statue of a rearing horse, similar to the Marly Horse statue there now.

Writing this book, I spent a lot of time in Joan's sitting room on the second floor. I would sit and think about her hiving herself off and claiming this chunk of the mansion for herself; apparently it was her favourite location. I think about her fighting in court with her sons over the estate Robert left to her in its entirety, being guardian to her grandchildren whose parents (her daughter Agnes and son-in-law James Harvey) had died of typhus, overseeing a business, and looking to marry her spinster daughters well. How I wish she'd kept a diary, but that was not the style of an Ayrshire lass such as Joan. She'd been widowed not long before Craigdarroch was finished. The last eighteen years of her life were difficult, as it seemed all Robert had created for the family was disappearing.

But even as the family fortune may have been slipping away, the Dunsmuirs left us a series of stories that show us how the lives of early European settlers were lived in Victoria and beyond. Some of them were gracious and well intentioned, some of them were real stinkers, and all of them were implicated in the larger project of European colonization of Vancouver Island, with its attendant exploitation, racism, sexism, and cruelty. Many of the stories in this book and elsewhere start with objects of the time, placed in a restored context. Objects are also the jumping-off point of the post-Dunsmuir stories this castle holds.

Some might say it's preposterous to think an overview of a massive story repository such as Craigdarroch Castle can be reduced to not even two dozen objects.

"In the particular is contained the universal," said James Joyce, noted in *Conversations with James Joyce* by Arthur Power, and I agree. We can view the wide expanse of meaning just as well, if not better, through the lens of a microscope as we can through that of a telescope. Why twenty-one objects? The number may seem a bit arbitrary, but it comes from the desire to vary the story of the castle's nineteenth-century beginnings and carry it forward to the current century for contemporary readers and for future generations, with each object used as a hook on which to hang a story and offer some context and tangential information.

Craigdarroch Castle houses more than just the stories of the shipping, railway, and coal baron (and western Canada's richest man, for a time) Robert Dunsmuir, his wife, Joan, and the fractious, fractured family he left behind. It also cradles the stories of the maimed and shell-shocked men sent home by the Empire after the Great War and cared for from 1919 to 1921 at Craigdarroch Military Hospital, as well as those of Victoria College, the Victoria Conservatory of Music, the Victoria school board, and the efforts of the Craigdarroch Castle Historical Museum Society.

It is a collection that allows us a peek into the lives of different people in a different time and provides us a bit of context for our lives in the twenty-first century. The objects range from world-class stained glass to tatting shuttles to a young officer's sabretache and spurs that speak of the military expectations of young men in the early twentieth century. Tales of class distinction are revealed through the examination of radiator brushes used by servants and the story of a piano ordered by one Dunsmuir brother and ultimately delivered to another brother in another city.

These objects can set our imaginations alight. Imagining an earlier time helps us create a better now and imagine a better future.

A VIEW OF THE
MAGNIFICENT
CENTRAL
STAIRCASE AT
CRAIGDARROCH

For their help with and support for this project, I would like to thank Craigdarroch Castle Executive Director John Hughes and Curator Bruce Davies, as well as castle staff, docents, fellow board members, and volunteers. I offer particular thanks to Margaret Klatt, who invited me to join the board years ago, to Taryn Boyd and Kate Kennedy of TouchWood Editions, and to my writing partner, Anita Lahey. I'm grateful to my friends who didn't cover their ears and run away when I said, "I learned the coolest thing today about the castle . . ." I'm particularly thankful to my late parents, Norm and Gerry Dann, who encouraged the history nut in me from the start. And I'm most grateful to Craigdarroch's historical denizens, who left behind so many great stories to uncover. And thanks always to my husband, Sam Bufalini, for his love and patient support.

I invite you to come and explore *Craigdarroch Castle in 21 Treasures.*

Moira Dann

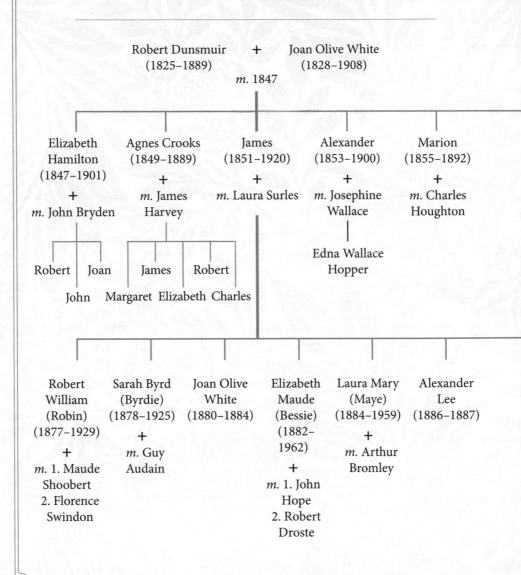

The
DUNSMUIR FAMILY TREE

Robert Dunsmuir   ✛   Joan Olive White
(1825–1889)   (1828–1908)

m. 1847

Elizabeth Hamilton (1847–1901)	Agnes Crooks (1849–1889)	James (1851–1920)	Alexander (1853–1900)	Marion (1855–1892)
✛	✛	✛	✛	✛
m. John Bryden	*m.* James Harvey	*m.* Laura Surles	*m.* Josephine Wallace	*m.* Charles Houghton

Robert   Joan   James   Robert

John   Margaret Elizabeth Charles

Edna Wallace Hopper

Robert William (Robin) (1877–1929)	Sarah Byrd (Byrdie) (1878–1925)	Joan Olive White (1880–1884)	Elizabeth Maude (Bessie) (1882–1962)	Laura Mary (Maye) (1884–1959)	Alexander Lee (1886–1887)
✛	✛		✛	✛	
m. 1. Maude Shoobert 2. Florence Swindon	*m.* Guy Audain		*m.* 1. John Hope 2. Robert Droste	*m.* Arthur Bromley	

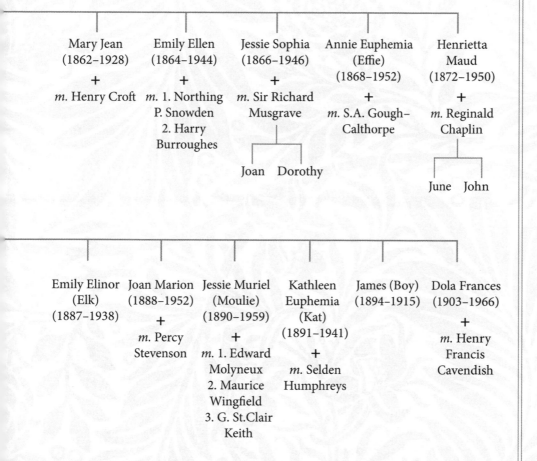

Mary Jean
(1862–1928)
+
m. Henry Croft

Emily Ellen
(1864–1944)
+
m. 1. Northing
P. Snowden
2. Harry
Burroughes

Jessie Sophia
(1866–1946)
+
m. Sir Richard
Musgrave

Joan　Dorothy

Annie Euphemia
(Effie)
(1868–1952)
+
m. S.A. Gough–
Calthorpe

Henrietta
Maud
(1872–1950)
+
m. Reginald
Chaplin

June　John

Emily Elinor
(Elk)
(1887–1938)

Joan Marion
(1888–1952)
+
m. Percy
Stevenson

Jessie Muriel
(Moulie)
(1890–1959)
+
m. 1. Edward
Molyneux
2. Maurice
Wingfield
3. G. St.Clair
Keith

Kathleen
Euphemia
(Kat)
(1891–1941)
+
m. Selden
Humphreys

James (Boy)
(1894–1915)

Dola Frances
(1903–1966)
+
m. Henry
Francis
Cavendish

BLACK FOREST-STYLE CARVED CLOCK

1

BLACK FOREST
CLOCK

I T'S A LARGE, CARVED WOODEN CLOCK featuring a magnificent stag and a doe beside him, with a fawn curled up on the ground beneath them. Between the two adult deer is a clock face with dark blue enamel Roman numerals, backed in white. The eyes of the stag and the doe are made of dark glass, and they sparkle in the hallway light. The stag's rack can be removed.

It's impressive, and it's one of the first things a visitor encounters when entering Craigdarroch Castle by way of the main hall, with the magnificent staircase to the left and, directly ahead, a carved sandstone fireplace.

The clock is on a mantelpiece backed by a hammered-metal panel above the fireplace. It's the first of several objects in the house carved most probably in linden wood and obtained in Europe.

The hearth sandstone is from Arizona, and the quote carved into the panel directly over the fireplace is from Shakespeare's *Troilus and Cressida*, which tells a story of the Trojan War from the *Iliad*. The quote is: "Welcome ever smiles and farewell goes out sighing." In more common parlance: I will grin when I welcome you, and when we say goodbye and you depart, I will sigh.

How did Joan Dunsmuir decide where to place the large, carved timepiece in her new home? It was notable in its size and popular motif and would have served to signal her wealth and status in society as well as her being up to date with popular styles.

It's thought Joan may have purchased the clock in 1890, when she decided to travel in Europe while waiting for the castle to be finished. She made this distaff "grand tour" with two of the unmarried daughters who were going to live with her, Jessie and Effie (as the second youngest, Annie Euphemia, was known). The daily progress of the Craigdarroch building project seemingly held little to no interest for Joan, widowed so suddenly in April 1889, and doubtless the girls were also still grieving their father's death.

Picture Joan (or one of her daughters) spotting this object in a shop, perhaps an atelier specializing in carvings of this type somewhere in Switzerland, where it and the other Black Forest-style carvings in the castle were likely acquired. Joan's life had not necessarily equipped her to judge the quality of the artisan's work, but she doubtless understood form and function and how to appreciate an appropriate marriage of the two. Perhaps knowing Queen Victoria liked this kind of decorative object, Joan may have chosen to follow the sovereign's taste.

The carving isn't signed, and the animals are red deer (not found in Canada but common in Europe—see sidebar), a common natural life motif of the day. The clock itself is believed to be older than the carved wood portion; the brass movement was made by Japy Frères & Company of France. There is an appropriately sized

How can Canada not have red deer when there is a city in Alberta by that very name? Red Deer (incorporated in 1913) is located on the Red Deer River, originally named Was-ka-soo (Elk) River by the Cree First Nation. The Scottish settlers misunderstood the translation and mistook the animals for the red deer they were used to hunting back home. The name stuck.

· · ·

ONE OF TWO BLACK FOREST-
STYLE WALL CARVINGS,
FOUND IN CRAIGDARROCH'S
DINING ROOM

hole in the carved base, and the clock was accessed from behind via a hinged door.

The clock is one of several Black Forest–style pieces Joan had in her home, which may well have been purchased on the same trip.

Another Black Forest–style item a Craigdarroch visitor encounters is the tall, elaborate hallstand or coat rack located in the Garden Entrance of the castle. It features a carved mother bear holding on to a tree trunk at the base of the stand and looking up at a cub farther up in the "branches" that were used as hooks for hats and cloaks. Around the mother bear's middle is a carved wooden branch that encircles umbrella handles, canes, and walking sticks. The carvings of the bodies of the cub and its mother are deeply cut, to represent fur. At her feet is a carved-out spot that would have held a metal tray, to catch rain dripping from umbrellas.

Joan may have bought this at the same time she bought the clock. Another Dunsmuir, son Alex, visited Switzerland on an 1894 trip to Europe and may have brought it back to Victoria.

The Black Forest style appears again in the dining room, where two wall carvings flank the fireplace and the windows at the end of the room. These deer plaques are reminiscent of deer being bled after a successful hunt; the animals are depicted hanging upside down, suspended by one rear leg. Disconcertingly, their eyes are open and the tongue hangs out. The carved animals are surrounded by carved ornamental leaves and acorns, and each panel is 123 centimetres high. Like the clock, the antlers on one panel are removable, but the "rack" is fixed on the other.

This kind of carving emerged in Switzerland in the early 1800s and grew in popularity across Europe. Much later in that century, carvers in Germany's Black Forest region started creating clocks with Swiss timekeeping mechanisms. It wasn't long before Swiss carvings of all types were known as Black Forest carvings and were a popular decorative style.

All the pieces were sold in the 1909 auction of Craigdarroch's contents following Joan's death. The hallstand was purchased by two brothers named Fields; Craigdarroch acquired it in 2003 from a Fields grandson. The hallstand had stayed on Vancouver Island and was a centrepiece in several Fields descendants' homes.

The clock had spent time in those homes as well. The castle reacquired the pieces when the Fields brothers' sister, Dr. Ruth (Fields) Brink, donated the clock to Craigdarroch in 1983.

2

WALNUT RENAISSANCE
REVIVAL CHAIRS

CONSIDER THIS SCENARIO: You have been invited (or maybe it feels more like summoned!) to Craigdarroch. Perhaps you're there to speak with the matriarch, Joan, or deal with one of the people who run the estate (maybe Robert Fitton, who does the gardening). Perhaps you've been asked for luncheon or tea with one of the Dunsmuir daughters in residence with Joan: Jessie, Effie, or Maud.

Perhaps you're guardian to a friend of young Master Robert Dunsmuir Harvey, Joan's grandson, and you've brought your charge to visit. The two young fellows are planning for an afternoon of riding or fencing (Robert was adept at both).

Robert Dunsmuir Harvey was just twelve when he was orphaned by typhoid fever and moved with his sister to live with his grandmother Joan at Craigdarroch. He lived at the castle for only five months before his grandmother sent him to boarding school back east: Trinity College School in Port Hope, Ontario. (Notable graduates include the brewer John Labatt, the business magnate Charles Bronfman, the journalist Peter Jennings, and the comedian Mark McKinney of *The Kids in the Hall*.)

Robert later went to the Royal Military College of Canada in Kingston, Ontario. Two months after graduating in 1899, he joined the Fourth (Queen's Own) Hussars, a British Army cavalry regiment. He quickly earned a promotion to lieutenant near the end of the following year. (Another lieutenant in this regiment was Winston Churchill.)

The Hussars were serving in India when Robert joined. It was a difficult assignment, and the regiment lost more than five hundred men to illness in just five years. In August 1901, Robert succumbed to liver disease at age twenty-three. His belongings were sent to his sister and grandmother in Victoria.

Or perhaps you're a suitor to Elizabeth Georgina Harvey, Joan's granddaughter. Elizabeth was the youngest child of Agnes Crooks Dunsmuir (Robert and Joan's second daughter) and James Harvey, a Nanaimo shopkeeper who had once been a miner. Elizabeth went with her brother Robert to live with their grandmother Joan after their mother died of typhoid fever in September 1889. This was just five months after Joan's husband and Agnes's father, Robert Dunsmuir, had died. Agnes was forty when she died. Her husband, James, also contracted typhoid; after Agnes died, he went to California to recover but died in Pasadena after just a few months.

Elizabeth Georgina spent most of her life in Nanaimo. In 1883, she moved with her parents and siblings into her grandparents' house, Ardoon, after Robert and Joan had moved to Victoria.

Built around 1876, Ardoon was the most opulent house in Nanaimo for a long time. Robert Dunsmuir conducted a lot of his business there and even hosted an overnight visit from the federal minister of railways, Sir Charles Tupper, when Robert sought the contract to build the Esquimalt and Nanaimo Railway.

"Lizzie" (one of her nicknames) finished growing up at Craigdarroch and married there in September 1903. The successful suitor was George Alan Kirk. The wedding photo features Elizabeth and the wedding party, including brother Robert, framed by the Craigdarroch porte cochère.

After they married, Elizabeth and George Kirk lived in a home on St. Charles Street called Riffham, designed by Francis Mawson Rattenbury, who also designed the BC Legislative Buildings and the Empress Hotel. (Rattenbury is best known for being driven

from Victoria by scandal and murdered by his second wife's lover in England, a crime for which she was acquitted but he was found guilty.) Elizabeth died in Victoria in September 1928.

IF A GENTLEMAN CALLER is invited to take a seat in the drawing room at Craigdarroch, it's the kind of chair that allows him to sit back, even cross his legs. Ladies would be more likely to be perched on the edge of their seat and sitting upright (a posture enforced by corseting) to sip their tea.

THIS WALNUT
RENAISSANCE
REVIVAL CHAIR
IS A CASTLE
ORIGINAL.

Facing page:

STAINED GLASS
WINDOW
REPRODUCTION
OF FREDERIC
LEIGHTON'S
ODALISQUE

These chairs are believed to have had pride of place in the drawing room, perhaps on either side of the stained glass window featuring a reproduction of the 1862 painting *Odalisque*, by Frederic Leighton, depicting the Greek myth of Leda and the Swan. (The original window was broken in 1927, when Craigdarroch housed Victoria College and rambunctious students sometimes threw snowballs. The current window is a reproduction.)

Or they may have lived in the billiard room on the third floor, where the Dunsmuir daughters, enjoying the game, spent a lot of their leisure time.

These chairs were Craigdarroch originals, sold at the 1909 auction following Joan's death. They returned home to the castle as a gift from Margaret Gertrude Tyson, mother of the Canadian country music legend Ian Tyson, who was born in Victoria and grew up in Duncan. He is best known as one-half of the renowned folk duo Ian & Sylvia. They had several crossover hits in the mid-1960s, including "Four Strong Winds," "You Were On My Mind," "Someday Soon," and "Summer Wages." The pair stopped performing together and divorced in the mid-1970s. They released *Ian & Sylvia: The Lost Tapes*, a collection of concert recordings, in 2019.

While the patterned blue fabric on the seats and the chair backs is not original, the frames were crafted in North America sometime between about 1870 and 1885. The fabric may not be original, but the chair would have been upholstered in something similarly luxurious.

Renaissance Revival was one of several revival styles popular in furniture during the Victorian era. This style was distinctive for elaborate, turned legs on the chairs as well as carved panels and edges. Walnut was a favourite wood during the Renaissance, and that preference is repeated here.

3

CRAIGDARROCH
KEYBOARDS

M USIC WAS OFTEN HEARD at Craigdarroch Castle. The
Dunsmuir family enjoyed listening to it as well as making
it. It was a feature when they entertained in the drawing room or
just spent time there together as a family, and certainly when they
hosted big events in the dance hall on the top floor.

Those events—such as the evening in 1894 when it's said 110
Victorians danced, and for which there is a gold-coloured dance
card with its own golden pencil (see page 113)—were among the
few socially sanctioned places where young men and women could
gather to meet, dance, and "court," with an eye toward matrimony.
There were also elaborate events held when some of the Dunsmuir
daughters came out and made their debut and were officially presented to society.

There are three pianos (among four keyboard instruments) in
Craigdarroch Castle. Each has a story, but the jewel in the crown
is the Steinway grand piano in the drawing room. Known as an
"art case" Steinway, the instrument has enjoyed regular, if not
continuous, use over the last century. The term refers to the elaborate designs that make the piano unique. The Dunsmuir art case
features floral swags and depictions of musical instruments and
notation along with bouquets.

This piano ended up with a different member of the Dunsmuir
family from the one who commissioned it from the Steinway

THE ART CASE
STEINWAY PIANO
ORDERED IN
NEW YORK BY
ALEXANDER
DUNSMUIR BUT
DELIVERED FROM
NEW YORK TO HIS
BROTHER JAMES

factory in New York City in 1898. It was Robert and Joan's younger son, Alexander Dunsmuir, who made the purchase for the grand California home he was building. When he bought it, he was in New York with the woman he called his wife but had yet to marry, to visit his stepdaughter, the actress Edna Hopper. But it wasn't long before Alexander's life was taken by the alcoholism that had long undermined his health. He died on January 31, 1900, in New York City on his honeymoon, and his wife, Josephine, died of cancer soon after.

His estate went in its entirety to his brother, James, so the piano was shipped to Victoria via Toronto from the Steinway facility in New York. It was a centrepiece at Burleith, the home of James and Laura Dunsmuir, and then it moved with them to Government House when James became lieutenant-governor in

1906. It later accompanied them to Hatley Castle when the family moved there in 1910. The greatest beneficiary of the instrument was Elinor Dunsmuir, the fifth-eldest daughter and seventh of James and Laura's surviving twelve children.

Elinor (or Elk, as she was known in the family) was a big talent and very smart, but the social constraints on women of the day didn't permit her to be part of the business or to do much else other than seek a good marriage. It's believed Elinor was gay, so the marry-well-and-have-heirs route didn't suit her. Her musical talent offered her a way out—talent she expressed on this piano. She spent much of her adulthood in Europe, studying and composing music for the stage and the ballet, and worked alongside greats such as Noël Coward. She also had a taste for gambling and did a lot of it in Monte Carlo.

The piano was used in performance of and to record some of Elinor's music in 2018, for a recording titled "La Riche Canadienne" (as Elinor was known in Monte Carlo).

The piano was auctioned off for $500 in 1939 after Laura Dunsmuir died. James and Laura's daughter, Muriel Dunsmuir, bought it back in 1953. It changed hands several more times before finding its forever home at the castle in 1985.

IN MANY WAYS, even more remarkable than the New York–crafted Steinway in the drawing room is the upright piano in the third-floor billiard room. Its pedigree is strictly local, with its metal frame having been cast at Albion Iron Works, partly owned by the Dunsmuir patriarch, Robert, and situated on Government Street. The piano builders were Charles Goodwin and G.W. Jordan, whose firm had a short life; they were thought to have crafted only thirteen pianos. This Goodwin and Jordan piano is believed to be one of very few still extant. It came to Craigdarroch in the late 1800s.

THE CASTLE'S
UPRIGHT
GOODWIN AND
JORDAN PIANO,
ONCE OWNED BY
THE DAUGHTER
OF SIR JAMES
DOUGLAS

Its other claim to fame is its ownership by Martha Harris, daughter of Sir James and Lady Amelia Douglas. Mrs. Harris left behind the vibrant correspondence she had with her father when she was in school in England. Later, after her parents died, she wrote a book, in which she shared the stories her Métis mother had told her when Harris was a youngster.

The third piano is the Collard & Collard in the fourth-floor dance hall that visitors are welcome to play.

Another keyboard worth noting is the melodeon in the dance hall. It came to Victoria from California in 1875, brought by Theophilus Elford, who established the Shawnigan Lake Lumber Company. The instrument was his wedding gift to his bride, Lillie Louisa Robertson, with whom he had six children. Lillie died in the Point Ellice Bridge collapse with their daughter, Grace Constance. The bridge collapsed on May 26, 1896, when a streetcar carrying 143 passengers on their way to celebrations of Queen Victoria's birthday fell into the Gorge Waterway. Fifty-five people died. An investigation found both the Consolidated Electric Railway Company and the Victoria City Council responsible for the accident, as the bridge was not constructed to handle the heavy weight of a streetcar and inspection techniques undermined the structure.

A melodeon is a type of reed organ that was popular in the latter part of the nineteenth century and into the twentieth. A keyboard wind instrument, it makes sound by drawing air (its suction created by a foot-pump bellows) over reeds. It's the suction that makes it different from a harmonium, which pumps air through reeds to make sound.

4

CRAIGDARROCH
STAINED GLASS

S TAINED GLASS WASN'T LIMITED to church windows around
the time Craigdarroch was built; "art glass" was fashionable
in houses both opulent and more humble.

At dawn each day, light begins to pour into Craigdarroch Castle
through a necklace of distinctive nineteenth-century art glass
windows, reflected from thousands of shining surfaces bevelled
into the glass. The effect is magical: thousands of sunbeams
shining through the jewel-toned panes of glass in the many
windows through which the light of the world reaches people
and objects. Using each individual surface as a canvas, it paints
impressionist images on skin and clothing and creates brightly lit
wallpaper in each room it enters.

The windows in the library are among the first a visitor sees
after entering the castle. A window over the fireplace features
a clear oval (with an expertly bevelled edge) in the centre that
highlights beautifully limned daisies to the left and the two
circular, ruby-hued "jewels" on either side at the midpoint. Ruby-
toned slices highlight the stained glass trim that encircles the
bevel, and flowing blue shapes evoke the water and the sky.

"Jewels" are inserts, often round, of ground, polished, co-
loured crystal, with a chiselled appearance. Light reflects from
their many facets, providing richness and depth of colour. The ribbon design outlining the window features interchanging ruby and

gold tones, and the outermost glass next to the wooden window
frame is a pale gold, bubbled glass, all colours reminiscent of sun-
set. The other windows in the library—three panes that frame the
bay window alcove—include a central transom panel of thistles.
The other two are bright floral designs, one of holly, the other of
bluebells, both additional allusions to the Scottish heritage of the
Dunsmuirs.

STAINED GLASS
CRAFTED IN SAN
FRANCISCO FOR
CRAIGDARROCH
CASTLE

The ribbon design, the bevelling, the floral motif, and the
use of faceted jewels of many shapes are repeated elsewhere in
the castle's remaining thirty-two windows. Forty-seven were
installed in 1890, but several disappeared from the castle after

Joan Dunsmuir's death in 1908, including those in the dining room, the sitting room, and a bathroom.

Other design elements distinctive to Craigdarroch stained glass windows are rope, knotted or kinked ribbon, and the scroll. But experts as well as armchair enthusiasts long puzzled over who might have brought these elements together in such exquisite designs. It took some real detective work to track down the artisan and manufacturer responsible. Because the work is unsigned (residential stained glass was rarely signed at that time), it wasn't possible to work backward from the designer to the art glass manufacturer. It was American-made, experts thought, although there were few clues to its origins.

The castle's architect, Arthur L. Smith of Portland, Oregon, included stained art glass in Craigdarroch's plans from the start. A newspaper story from 1890 notes A.H. Andrews & Company was asked to supply "windows" along with woodwork for the castle's interior. It was long believed that the art glass must have come from an eastern studio such as Tiffany. Or, more likely, a studio somewhere in the Midwest, probably Chicago. Or perhaps Povey of Portland, a leading art glass maker in the Pacific Northwest for the better part of thirty years, from about 1890 to about 1920.

The design clues included Celtic knots and curved windows, repeated in art glass in other mid-nineteenth-century "bonanza" mansions. Another clue was the singular artistry and three-dimensionality of each creation. Many of Craigdarroch's panels break the rules of standard Victorian art glass, such as using a sinuous rope effect in the image framing within the glass itself,

AN UNUSUAL PORTRAIT OF SIR WALTER RALEIGH IN STAINED
GLASS IS A FOCAL POINT OF THE CASTLE'S SMOKING ROOM.

as opposed to the standard straight-edged framing of the period.
Sometimes the image seems to drop off the edge of the art glass
image, uncontained by the frame. One set of Craigdarroch windows
features free-floating flowers on a background with a basket-
weave texture.

There are two panels that are neither floral nor strictly decorative. One is the profile of Sir Walter Raleigh featured in the
smoking-room window; the other is the reproduction in glass of
Frederic Leighton's painting *Odalisque*. Both convey the extent of
design talent and art glass manufacturing abilities available to the
artisans who created the Craigdarroch windows.

However, daisies were the clue that broke the mystery open.
The daisies in the window over the fireplace in the castle's library
are almost an exact match with daisies found in the bedroom

window of Sarah Winchester, widow of the fire-arms maker William Wirt Winchester, at the family mansion in San Jose, California. But how could one flower have cracked the case?

Art glass producers of the day built their reputations on being able to provide distinctive, exclusive designs to their clients. They were fiercely protective of their original work, so distinctive daisies pointed to a particular window maker.

It was timing, particular design elements, and clever sleuthing by BC historian Jim Wolf that, in 2019, finally revealed the creators of the Craigdarroch windows: John Mallon of Pacific Art Glass in San Francisco was the manufacturer, and Harry Ryle Hopps, who worked for Mallon, was the designer.

John Mallon was originally from New York. With his family, he was on his way to BC and the Fraser River gold rush, but friends in San Francisco dissuaded him. He started his art glass firm in 1858. Pacific Art Glass became the largest art glass maker west of the Rockies. He employed thirty-six men with three designers working full-time, creating most of the art glass in San Francisco mansions that were built before the earthquake in 1906.

THE STAINED GLASS REPRODUCTION OF *ODALISQUE*

Harry Ryle Hopps was one of the Pacific Art Glass designers and also had his own firm where he worked in lithography, designing items such as a First World War recruitment poster. His work in art glass is evident in the stained glass dome atop the rotunda in the Neiman Marcus store in San Francisco, as well as the "new" Palace Hotel, rebuilt after the quake.

Patience and curiosity in the twenty-first century led to a nineteenth-century mystery being solved.

5

MARLY HORSE
on PEDESTAL

DETAIL OF
THE BRONZE
MARLY HORSE
SCULPTURE

I F A VISITOR were to have joined the Dunsmuir daughters in the drawing room to read and maybe sew and make music—as they are shown doing in the only extant photograph of Dunsmuir family members at Craigdarroch around 1895—that visitor would have met a Marly Horse.

It is an evocative piece of cast bronze sculpture, standing almost sixty centimetres high, of a groom, naked to the waist, barely restraining a rearing horse by the reins. The visitor would have seen its burnished surface and the movement in the metal, the light glinting on its golden-greenish patina. Despite its warm appearance, it would be cool to the touch.

Such a sculpture is featured in the rare photograph noted, on the right-hand side. The Dunsmuir women are seated near one of the two Corinthian columns that mark the middle of the long rectangular room. Joan's granddaughter Elizabeth Harvey is seen with her aunts Jessie, Effie, and Maud, and a rearing Marly Horse is situated high up and to the right in the photograph. A piano is visible in the background. Effie is pictured playing the banjo, Elizabeth is reading, and Jessie is playing a guitar or maybe a ukulele.

The photo appeared on page 6 in the Victoria *Daily Colonist* newspaper on April 25, 1948. The newspaper photo credit was given to Mrs. John Hope, the married name of Bessie (Elizabeth Maud) Dunsmuir, another of Joan's granddaughters. The original has never been found.

We know a Marly Horse sculpture was part of the original decor of the house because it's featured so clearly in this photograph. Records show that the Dunsmuirs owned two such sculptures. The identical Marly Horses are miniature representations of a pair of horses (sculpted in marble by Guillaume Coustou during the reign of Louis XV) that once graced the Château de Marly outside Paris and later stood at the entrance to the Champs-Élysées before being moved to the Louvre museum in 1984.

When would the Dunsmuirs have purchased such bronze sculptures? It's not certain, but it might have been on the trip Joan and two of the daughters took not long after Robert died. Robert himself visited Paris in 1882, so he might have purchased them. Several Dunsmuir daughters visited the Continent by themselves

THE BRONZE PEDESTAL BENEATH THE
MARLY HORSE SPENT SOME OF ITS LIFE
AS AN ELECTRIC LAMP.

and could have brought them home. The Marly Horse currently on display is a reproduction.

The gaze of anyone visiting might have slid down from the statue to see the ornate pedestal, also crafted in bronze, which held aloft the Marly Horse sculpture in the drawing room. It depicts a curly-haired cherub, or putto, with bare arms and chest, holding a pillow on his head. The pillow is actually the rectangular metal surface where the Marly Horse stands. Where the cherub's legs should be is a single, decoratively cast column, and at its base are four feet featuring cast lion's heads. The pedestal is just under 110 centimetres tall.

The pedestal was sold at the 1909 auction following Joan's death. For many years, it stood at the entrance to an antique shop located in the lobby of the Empress Hotel.

It was then sold to a private collector in Oak Bay, who drilled a hole in it, threaded wiring through, and turned it into an electric lamp base. Craigdarroch Castle reacquired it in a 1993 auction in Victoria.

Both the Marly Horse sculpture and the pedestal on which it stands were crafted using the lost wax (*cire perdue*) method of production. The artist sculpts the piece in wax and cuts the wax sculpture in pieces. Then a plaster mould is made of each piece. The pieces are assembled and then hot wax is used again, poured in to create a thin wax layer inside the plaster mould. This is repeated until the artist achieves the desired thickness of the wax. The wax sections are then pulled from the plaster form and the original wax figure is re-created, its hollow core then filled with plaster. Pins are inserted to hold the plaster form in place, and wax channels are created to funnel molten metal and let gas escape later on, when the molten bronze is poured. But first, still *another* soft plaster form is created around the wax figure. This

plaster mould is fired in a kiln; the wax melts and drains from the form. The components of bronze, mostly copper and tin, are heated to about 1,000 degrees Celsius. The liquid metal is then poured into the plaster mould. After the molten metal has cooled, the plaster is chipped away, and the bronze sculpture is revealed. Details are smoothed out, and a patina made of wax and acid applied, to give the bronze that burnished golden-green effect.

The apparent photographer of the Dunsmuir girls making music in the Craigdarroch drawing room that day in 1895 was Elizabeth Maud, better known as Bessie. The third-eldest daughter of Robert and Joan's eldest son, James, and his wife, Laura, she would have been about thirteen when she took the photo. A beautiful child, a true Dunsmuir, she went on to become a beautiful young woman, noted to be round and not too tall. She married John Alexander Hope, an aristocratic young man who served as a major in the Canadian Scottish Regiment. She walked down the aisle on April 15, 1908, at St. George's, Hanover Square, London, with none other than the Canadian prime minister, Sir Wilfrid Laurier, taking her father's role. (Coincidentally, Canada's first prime minister, Sir John A. Macdonald, was married to his second wife, Agnes, in that same church on February 16, 1867.)

Bessie loved the theatre, and during the First World War she organized benefit stage events in London. She had a stunning success on May 11, 1917, when she produced the Canadian Matinee, starring her very own sister Muriel, known as Moulie in the family. In the audience were King George V and Queen Mary, Queen Alexandra (mother of King George and widow of King Edward VII), and another Canadian prime minister, Sir Robert Borden.

Bessie and John had two children, but their marriage ended in 1923. She did a lot of travelling and undertook a second marriage to the much younger heir to the Droste Dutch chocolate fortune, Robert. It didn't last, and she went back to using her previous married name, Mrs. John Hope. Bessie bought a home in Portugal, and that's where she died at age eighty-one.

6

PHOTOGRAPHS OF HENRIETTA MAUD *and* MARION JOAN

THIS PHOTO OF HENRIETTA MAUD DUNSMUIR, the youngest daughter of Robert and Joan, was taken circa 1931, when she was fifty-nine. She was very glamorous, with marcelled hair and a fur collar on an expensive jacket. Quite a contrast to the photo taken of Henrietta Maud around the time she moved into Craigdarroch in 1890, when she was eighteen. That photo is sepia toned, and so she looks older even though she was younger.

Born when Joan was forty-five, Maud, as she was known, was the youngest of ten children, and the youngest of eight girls. She grew up in Victoria and Nanaimo. After Robert, her father, died in 1889, she moved with her mother and two other unmarried sisters (Jessie and Effie) into Craigdarroch when it was finally finished in September 1890.

PORTRAIT OF HENRIETTA
MAUD DUNSMUIR, C. 1931

PORTRAIT OF
HENRIETTA
MAUD
DUNSMUIR,
C. 1890

It's clear Joan regarded the eighteen-room castle as a showcase for a widow's wealth and a lure for potential husbands for her daughters. It was certainly the fulcrum for Victoria's high society and the focus of much of the social season for many years. And while the castle may have succeeded in attracting more aristocratic suitors, Maud's brothers both noted that the higher-class a gentleman was, the less likely he would be able to support himself.

But the castle bait worked. Maud's sister Jessie was the first to marry a titled Irish gentleman: Sir Richard John Musgrave. Her wedding at Craigdarroch was legendary. Her marriage into Irish aristocracy gave her an entree into court life in London and Dublin. Maud and Effie both visited Jessie in Dublin and found it both entertaining and romantically intriguing because of the large number of British Army officers stationed there. It wasn't long before Maud, described in Terry Reksten's *The Dunsmuir Saga* as "Lady Musgrave's pretty sister," found herself at the altar, marrying Reggie Chaplin, an officer in the Tenth Royal Hussars.

But long before that, when Maud was still a maiden, she accompanied her mother on a tour of Europe, waiting for Craigdarroch's completion after her father died, when she would have her own lovely room in the castle.

Some of the objects in what's considered Maud's room at Craigdarroch answer questions as well as ask questions about how an upper-class single lady in Victorian Victoria would have lived. A bed, a vanity, a writing desk: the room's essentials. A button hook to help button shoes and boots, a glove stretcher, a jar with a hole

in the lid called a hair receiver: accoutrements of a lady's life back in the day.

A different kind of Dunsmuir portrait is in the castle library: it is that of Maud's older sister Marion. It's right next to a letter Effie wrote to Mrs. O'Reilly, who lived over on the Gorge at Point Ellice House. It's a thank you to her for flowers she sent after Marion died in 1892.

Marion's story was sad but not unusual at the time. She was wooed and won by Charles Frederick Houghton, an Anglo-Irish fellow from Dublin who started out at seventeen as a soldier in the British Army. It looked promising; he became a captain before he was twenty-four years old, but then he changed tack, sold his commission, and bought land in BC, near Okanagan Lake.

He didn't find what he wanted working his four hundred hectares and signed up when Governor James Douglas sent out the call for volunteers for a reconnaissance mission, investigating stories of a gold discovery. It wasn't long before Douglas found Houghton to be incompetent.

Yet, thanks to an even more incompetent returning officer, Houghton was acclaimed to one of the six seats BC gained in Canada's House of Commons when the province joined Confederation in 1871. He changed tack again when he discovered BC would become a Canadian military district requiring a militia, moving on from political life to become a lieutenant colonel charged with organizing the province's militia forces.

In 1869, Houghton had started living common-law with a First Nations woman, Sophie N'kwala, and they'd had two children. Sophie's grandfather was a chief, and he'd married the two himself. It was common for soldiers, miners, and fur traders to set up house with Indigenous or Métis women. It was known as having a "country wife."

When Houghton's new job meant he had to move to Victoria, he decided to leave Sophie, daughter Marie, and son Edward, his Okanagan family, behind. Marie, in a document she later wrote for the Okanagan Historical Society, said, "We went to live with my grandmother and my mother died of a broken heart."

As bad a soldier as Houghton was, he was a lucky one. He led the militia from Victoria to help (successfully) put down a possible riot at a colliery owned by Robert Dunsmuir in Wellington, near Nanaimo. Not long after, he was invited to the boss's house, Ardoon, for dinner. There he met Marion, the boss's daughter.

For Marion, time was ticking away. She met Houghton, fifteen years older than she was, when he came to the house in Nanaimo—and he started to court her. He ultimately persuaded her to be his bride, and they married in March 1879. Then they settled into their own home. Did Marion know about the country family?

Marion and her new husband had lived there barely a year when Houghton was sent to Manitoba, where the government troops were in conflict with the Métis. Houghton couldn't wait to see some action. Prime Minister John A. Macdonald asked his son, Hugh, a lawyer in Winnipeg, his thoughts on Houghton as a militia leader. They were noted in a letter dated July 8, 1884, in the Macdonald Papers at the BC Archives: "Col. Houghton is getting along fairly well as Deputy Adjutant General. . . . I should say that he has plenty of pluck and determination and would make a capital fighting officer, but I must frankly admit I don't think he would be a capable commander as he has not much head and still less judgment."

Houghton didn't do well in any of the battles. His commanding officer, quoted in *Telegrams of the North-West Campaign, 1885*, edited by Desmond Morton and Reginald Roy, said: "Lt. Col. Houghton is absolutely useless, and I wish I could find some excuse to get rid of him." He must have found one, for Houghton was sent to Montreal. Marion wasn't doing well; her health was faltering. He brought Marion back to Victoria in 1891 and the couple lived at Craigdarroch, but not for long.

Marion died at age thirty-five, one day before Valentine's Day, February 13, 1892. After her death the Dunsmuirs weren't interested in keeping Houghton in the family (as was the case with most Dunsmuir sons-in-law).

This allowed Houghton to reconnect with his "country" family, and his daughter, Marie, joined him to live in Montreal. In 1898, Houghton was diagnosed with cancer, and he died in August of that year. The obituary spoke of his military career but never mentioned he'd once been married to a Dunsmuir.

7

DINING ROOM TABLE
and CHAIRS

I T'S AN EVENT AT CRAIGDARROCH, one that involves dinner. After a low-key beginning to the evening, possibly in the drawing room or the billiard room upstairs, guests are ushered into the dining room. It's a stunning salon, reminiscent of a time when a formal dinner was an almost daily event. At dinner, Joan Dunsmuir would be at the head of her dining table for a *Downton Abbey*–style formal meal, replete with staff serving from the left and clearing from the right.

Made of red oak stained a golden oak tint, the dining room table had fourteen matching chairs (two with arms) and a chaise longue as part of the original set. The table could be extended with seven leaves, organized by Roman numerals cut into the wood to help match up the dowels and the holes on each leaf. A hand crank and a steel extension screw underneath the tabletop further managed the table leaves. The table skirt and legs are intricately carved, and each foot houses a double-wheeled brass caster. It was a centrepiece of life at the castle from 1890 until Joan died in 1908.

The dining room's built-in sideboard is located between the mystery door that leads to a 1.2-metre drop outside and the door to the serving pantry and kitchen. The far end of the room is distinguished by another stunning stained glass window over the fireplace, a placement made possible by another bent-flue chimney. The window and hearth configuration is bracketed by

two additional windows, which also feature stained glass, as well as location- and purpose-built shutters.

Diners can gaze upon paintings featured on the walls, including two landscapes by Frederick Schafer. One is called *Mountain of the Holy Cross* and depicts a peak in Colorado, west of Denver. It's unknown if any Dunsmuir family member ever saw this mountain while travelling. The second is an evocation of evening light on Mount Tamalpais, in Northern California. Called *Evening on Mt. Tamalpais, California*, it depicts a view visible from San Francisco, a city most Dunsmuirs visited at one time or another, and where Robert and Joan's second son, Alexander, lived and oversaw Dunsmuir interests in the United States. Joan may have purchased this painting herself at an auction of Schafer's work held in Vancouver in 1891.

Robert considered Alexander a better businessman than his older brother, James, and put him in charge of the US coal sales and shipping. Alex built a mansion in 1899 called Dunsmuir House

THE CASTLE'S ORIGINAL RED OAK DINING TABLE AND CHAIRS

THE FREDERICK
SCHAFER PAINTING
FEATURED IN THE
CRAIGDARROCH
DINING ROOM,
*EVENING ON
MT. TAMALPAIS,
CALIFORNIA*

in what is now Oakland, California. It was to be a wedding gift to his long-time lover, Josephine Wallace. While she was officially his landlady, they lived as man and wife for years but didn't marry because of a threat from Alex's parents to disown him if he married Josephine, a divorcee. Alex finally did marry her in 1900, just weeks before he died of alcoholism in New York City. Josephine lived in the beautiful home he built for her for a short while after Alex died, but then she died, as well, in 1901. The home is now called the Dunsmuir Hellman Historic Estate.

A third painting, by Albert Bredow, depicts a sixteenth-century procession of men in religious garb moving through the cloister in Germany's Magdeburg Cathedral.

Joan would sit and dine with her marriageable daughters and members of the Victoria-area gentry, maybe some suitable young military officers. Before long, also invited were impoverished (but land-rich and titled) Anglo-Irish nobility Joan hoped would join her family via marriage and imbue the Dunsmuir name with renewed respectability.

Joan wasn't shy about holding events that demanded the silver, using good food, wine, and ostentatious wealth to lure respectable husband material into the slipstream of her spinster daughters. It worked with Sir Richard John Musgrave, a titled but indebted member of the Anglo-Irish aristocracy, whose passion for salmon fishing, in addition to an uncle with a sheep farm on Salt Spring Island, had led him to Vancouver Island—and to dining at Joan Dunsmuir's.

It wasn't long before Joan attached hundreds of thousands of dollars to her daughter Jessie, Sir Richard shed a fiancée in London, and the betrothal and imminent wedding was announced of Jessie Sophia and the fifth Baronet of Tourin.

JESSIE DUNSMUIR AND HER BRIDAL ATTENDANTS

SILVER SERVICE

The Dunsmuir silver is a long-term loan from the Royal BC Museum for many years. Craigdarroch Castle built a special display cabinet, reclaimed the silver, and made a star of the already stellar reproduction of the ground-floor dining room.

It's a formal dinner at the castle. It's not hard to imagine the faint, clean, lemony scent from the waxed wood of the many-leaved table and the pressed linen tablecloth covering it. The sparkling clean china place settings sit before the place cards, framed on three sides by the polished, glinting Dunsmuir silver.

The pattern is traditional, with a scroll-style *D* marking the handle of each knife, fork, spoon, and serving implement. A diner could feel the sterling heft in the hand when a fork was picked up to spear a bite, or a knife to cut it demurely.

The wedding was, to quote the September 24, 1891 *Daily Colonist* newspaper, "the most fashionable and brilliant witnessed in Victoria for many months." There were three hundred guests, and Jessie had as many as thirty attendants, including flower girls.

It's not unlike the *Downton Abbey* story. Consider the way, in *Downton Abbey*, Lord Robert Crawley, Earl of Grantham, married the American Cora Levinson. She happened to have a sizable dowry, thanks to the fortune earned by her New York family in dry goods. Cora's money helped save Downton Abbey, and marrying into the British aristocracy gave Cora's family the respect it craved after years of being regarded as "nouveau riche."

The Dunsmuirs were considered similarly nouveau riche and were deemed a bit gauche by some in Victoria's upper strata of society because they'd made their fortune mining coal. And Robert hadn't inherited the coal operation; he'd come to Canada and worked as a miner for the Hudson's Bay Company, as he had worked as a miner in his home in Scotland. Robert Dunsmuir was anti-union and an eager strikebreaker. He ran for office and was elected to the provincial legislature, as the member of the legislative assembly for Nanaimo. He lobbied for land and money to build the Esquimalt and Nanaimo Railway—and got both from Canada's new federal government, led by Sir John A. Macdonald.

No matter what anyone might say, nothing beats piles of money to buy your family's place in society—and the Dunsmuirs had piles and piles of money, even after Robert died and Joan spent a great deal of what was left to secure good marriages for her remaining daughters (remember, she had eight of them).

And lots of money could buy beautiful furniture for the new castle. The magnificent centrepiece of the room, the dining table and chairs, was purchased new for Craigdarroch in 1890. After myriad dinners were hosted at Craigdarroch, the table was sold in the 1909 auction to a Victoria saloon owner named Henry Siebenbaum. At 152.5 by 421.7 centimetres (with all seven leaves installed), the table was too big for the dining room in his home at 1109 Catherine Street in Victoria, so he cut two leaves from it to

THE DINING ROOM TABLE SET FOR A HOLIDAY DINNER

make it fit. Thank goodness he kept the pieces along with the seven additional leaves that came with the table.

After Siebenbaum died in 1942, his effects went to his brother in Port Townsend, Washington, and his great-nephew later inherited them. Craigdarroch Castle acquired the set, including six of the original chairs, from him in 2003. The original chaise longue has never been found. The castle glued back into place the pieces of the table that had been cut out for length and commissioned a furniture maker in Sooke, BC, to reproduce the missing chairs and chaise longue.

8

DRAWING *by* ANNIE EUPHEMIA (EFFIE)

A DUNSMUIR DAUGHTER—moneyed, well dressed, somewhat educated, possibly bored, looking to marry well—did get an education about things such as needlework (see chapter 21, "Tools for Ladylike Pursuits: Tatting Shuttles") and art. Not just art history—she was able to learn about drawing and painting. And Annie Euphemia, or Effie, had some artistic talent that was revealed early.

Jessie's marriage to Sir Richard Musgrave had opened up a world of possibilities when it came to her sisters getting married, with the social access she had to Dublin's top-tier society. Jessie threw a ball in Dublin in the spring of 1898, an event where she and her youngest sister, Maud, played host to the elite of the city. There were lots of young officers at these events in Dublin, and sure enough, a couple of months later, Maud married one of them.

On June 8, 1898, little sister Maud married Reginald (Reggie) Spencer Chaplin, an officer of the Tenth Royal Hussars; he was aide-de-camp to the commander of Her Majesty's forces in Ireland, Lord (Frederick) Roberts.

When Effie visited Dublin, she appeared to burn the candle at both ends: cycling, riding, hunting all day, and then dancing the night away. Her mother grew quite worried at reports of Effie's manic spree and asked her to come home, but Effie defied her and stayed on, saying she'd never had so much fun.

Just two years after her sister's big day, Effie had her own: On February 27, 1900, she walked down the aisle herself, with Commander Somerset Arthur Gough-Calthorpe of the Royal Navy. The second son of the seventh Baron Calthorpe, he was judged by one officer to have "not one ounce of magnetism," (as quoted in *The Naval War in the Mediterranean 1914–18* by Paul G. Halpern) although he did have a home on the Isle of Wight and would serve as King George V's naval aide-de-camp in 1924. The couple had no children.

The sombreness of Effie's wedding in St. George's, Hanover Square, in London was in contrast to her sister Maud's event two years previous, which had been full of the titled and wealthy. Effie's wedding date fell not long after her uncle Alex had died in New York of chronic alcoholism.

Effie was a young woman when she moved into Craigdarroch with her grandmother, sisters, and orphaned cousins. It has been said she was the prettiest of all the Dunsmuir girls. The pencil-on-paper drawing of the character Goody Two-Shoes was a picture she had drawn when she was younger (probably around twelve) and still lived in Nanaimo and went to St. Ann's Convent and School. She gave it to her friend Maggie Beck, and Maggie's granddaughter made a gift of it to the castle.

Books written just for children were a rarity when John Newbery published *The History of Little Goody Two-Shoes* in 1765. It tells the story of the orphan brother and sister Tommy and Margery Meanwell. They are poor and hungry and dressed in rags; Margery has only one shoe. A kind gentleman provides her with a pair of shoes, and she goes on to make good: She grows up and becomes a schoolteacher and then meets and marries a local man of means. Her newfound riches enable her to help others, even more than the kind gentleman who gave her a pair of shoes had helped her. It's a moralistic tale, teaching that virtue and hard work are rewarded and that money is best used in the service of others. Calling someone a "goody two-shoes" is now a put-down, but it wasn't always.

Little Goody Two Shoes

AN ORIGINAL DRAWING OF GOODY TWO-SHOES DONE BY YOUNG EFFIE DUNSMUIR

DETAIL OF EFFIE'S SIGNATURE
ON HER GOODY TWO-SHOES
DRAWING

St. Ann's Convent and School in Nanaimo got started in 1877, with some twenty-nine students attending—including Dunsmuir daughters Effie, Emily, and Maud, who went to the convent to learn English, arithmetic, drawing, and needlework—and two members of the Sisters of St. Ann giving classes in the home of the town's priest, Father Lemmens (later bishop of Vancouver Island). The Sisters of St. Ann had come to BC from Quebec (their mother house remains in Lachine, Quebec), arriving in Victoria in 1858 to start a school. They also cared for the sick.

The school in Nanaimo got its own building (the Presbyterian Robert Dunsmuir contributed fifty dollars to its construction) within a couple of years of the first two sisters arriving. The first convent burned along with the adjacent parish church in 1910 and was rebuilt while the children went to school in Ladysmith; the new school opened in August 1911. Another fire in 1955 did serious damage to the school, but St. Ann's overcame that, too, with new wiring in place. The St. Ann's Convent Parish School closed for good in June 1966.

In 1896 Effie, her sister Jessie (Lady Musgrave), and her friend Kathleen O'Reilly of Point Ellice House travelled to Ireland. Kathleen's letters reveal the extravagant lifestyle Effie and her sisters were living. In a letter following her presentation to the Lord Lieutenant of Ireland, Lord Cadogan, at Dublin Castle, Kathleen wrote,

"There were some magnificent dresses and diamonds, and some beautiful women. . . . Effie had a costly and elaborate gown of blue and silver." (Kathleen's letters are part of the O'Reilly family collection at the BC Archives.)

Kathleen's letters offer the first hint of Effie's mental illness: "The Dublin Court Journal said Lady Musgrave and her beautiful Canadian sister [Effie] were among the best dressed at the first drawing room. . . . Effie has simply been on the go since we came here. . . . She is not looking well. . . . She is as thin as a knife. The people here seem to think she is rather mad to hunt all day and dance all night, any spare time being filled up by bicycling, at homes, or skating!! . . . Her appearance is quite sad and Jessie is worried about her."

Unfortunately, the potential problems hinted at during Effie's manic, apparently sleepless whirl in Dublin society while visiting with her sister Jessie as a young woman ended up coming true. Friends expressed concern that she was wearing herself out, and her mother urged her to come home to Victoria, but Effie was having too good a time. It was by staying overseas that she met Gough-Calthorpe, thirty-six. When they married in 1900, her brother-in-law Sir Richard Musgrave walked her down the aisle in London.

Her husband was known as Arthur in the family; he was a diplomat, a naval attaché. Apparently, while Arthur was on assignment in St. Petersburg during some unrest, Effie was in her carriage and found herself caught up in a riot. The family story says a severed human hand came flying into her carriage window and landed in Effie's lap. Arthur brought her home to Victoria shortly after, and the family believed this trauma incited Effie's descent into intractable mental illness.

Not even ten years after her wedding, Effie was in an asylum in England, having been declared irrevocably insane after Arthur applied for a certificate of lunacy. She spent more than forty years institutionalized, apparently pretty much forgotten by her family, and died in 1952 at a nursing home on the Isle of Wight. Arthur had predeceased her fifteen years earlier. Her money was almost gone.

9

PAINTINGS *by* FREDERICK SCHAFER

NYONE WHO ENTERED Craigdarroch on day one in 1890, like Joan and the three daughters who moved into the castle with her, might look at the expanse of wall space and wonder: Where do you even start?

Craigdarroch has been the subject of myriad paintings in many styles, and with several floors of wall space, it also houses a great deal of art.

Frederick Schafer is one of the best-represented artists in the castle. His oil on canvas titled *The California Alps* is prominently displayed in the library. In the dining room, an 1890 Schafer oil titled *Mountain of the Holy Cross* depicts that Rocky Mountain peak in Colorado. Also in the dining room is another 1890 Schafer piece, *Evening on Mt. Tamalpais, California*. Mount Tamalpais is just north of San Francisco, in California's Marin County (see page 58).

An arresting Schafer is on the wall in Joan Dunsmuir's sitting room: *Morning, Mt. Shasta, Ca.* This was one of the paintings listed in the auction catalogue; it reappeared years later at Kilshaw's Auctioneers, supporting the belief that much of what was auctioned off from the castle in September 1909 didn't travel too far, and much of it remained on Vancouver Island. The painting depicts two snow-covered mountain peaks, their lines softened behind mist appearing to rise from the ground. There are several evergreens

prominent in the foreground in addition to a number of First Nations people on a path in the centre foreground of the canvas.

This painting shows what the view of Mount Shasta would have been like from high ground in a town called Dunsmuir, California. This nomenclature came about when Alex Dunsmuir, Robert and Joan's younger son and the Dunsmuir coal and shipping dynasty's man in San Francisco, travelled through the small northern California town in 1888. He thought it was just beautiful and sought to have it named after his family. His offer to build a fountain in exchange for the town's naming rights sealed the deal, and the fountain still functions in the city of about 1,575 inhabitants.

The Dunsmuirs owned a number of other Schafers; there were eight listed as sold in the 1909 castle contents auction, but the canvas *Autumn in the Adirondacks*, currently in the dining room, wasn't on that list.

Frederick Schafer was an American painter who specialized in Western landscapes. Born in Braunschweig, Germany, in 1839, he came to America in 1876. He is considered a painter of the Rocky Mountain or San Francisco school. He worked mostly in oil on canvas and concentrated on impressionist-influenced but realist landscapes of dramatic vistas found mostly on the west coast of North America. His work still commands the interest of collectors worldwide.

Why so many paintings of American landscapes? Many of those seen in Schafer's paintings would have been known by members of the Dunsmuir family from their travels to Northern California to look after their business interests in San Francisco.

10

JAMES DUNSMUIR'S TELESCOPE

WHILE THIS TELESCOPE has a place of honour in the Craigdarroch Castle third-floor billiard room, it started out being used by the eldest Dunsmuir son, James, at his magnificent home, Hatley Castle, in what is now Colwood.

James (or any Dunsmuir) using the telescope here would be looking out over Victoria from Craigdarroch to the Strait of Juan de Fuca or beyond to the Saanich Peninsula and Mount Douglas.

James was very comfortable in Hatley Castle, which he built while living at his Burleith estate on the Gorge.

While he became a captain of industry, a politician, and a statesman, all he really wanted was to live the life of a squire, with land to groom and roam and rivers to fish.

He kept an eye on Hatley's location in Colwood, about twenty kilometres out of town and near the Esquimalt Lagoon. There was worry Laura wouldn't want to live so far away from town, as her social life was crucial in trying to arrange good marriages for her eight daughters. But when he took her out to see the location, she was quite taken with the view and the sound of the water. The view he would have experienced through his telescope from Hatley would encompass the waters of Esquimalt Lagoon, the Strait of Juan de Fuca and the vessels travelling on it, and the Olympic Mountains across the strait in the state of Washington.

Laura also recognized that James had done his duty to the Dunsmuir family and to the province of British Columbia, and now, he should be able to do as he wished.

James bought the land upon which an enviable estate had stood (destroyed by fire) and kept purchasing land as it became available in the environs. He ended up with 320 hectares, having spent about $1.35 million in twenty-first-century dollars.

He wanted to build a medieval castle, with enough land surrounding to raise horses and sheep and dairy cattle. Laura wanted room for the family and to be able to entertain. They chose to work with the renowned architect Samuel Maclure.

Maclure had designed and built many family estate houses and mansions in Victoria, but none as big as that desired by James and Laura.

The design featured a Norman-style keep and additional east and west wings in the Tudor Revival style, popular in Victorian times. Hatley was built using granite from the estate and sandstone from the nearby Gulf Islands. The blocks of stone of random shapes and sizes with smooth mortar between is called "snail creep." The roof slate travelled by ship from northern England and the cast iron downspouts came from Glasgow. Hatley is a 3,700-square-metre building in stone; construction started in 1908 and finished in 1910. To complete a building job of this ilk, with such fine, skilled workmanship in about eighteen months is nothing short of remarkable.

James used this telescope aboard his yacht, TSSY (stands for twin-screw steam yacht) *Dolaura*, named for his youngest daughter, Dola, and his wife, Laura. It was built in 1908 in Paisley, Scotland,

THE *DOLAURA*
WAS LUXURIOUSLY
APPOINTED.

at the Fleming and Ferguson shipyard. After James died in 1920, the vessel had several owners before being scrapped in Italy in 1951. The yacht, 58 metres long with a beam of 10 metres, had been designed in Victoria but built of steel in Scotland. Initially coal fired, it was capable of a speed of fourteen knots. During the Second World War, the ship was requisitioned by the Admiralty and renamed HMS *Valena*. It played a role in Operation Neptune, the first portion of the D-Day invasion.

The 203-centimetre-long brass telescope, made in France by A. Bardou and sold by A. Chevalier, might have been thought of little use aboard a private yacht because of its size and the potential "tippiness" of a non-naval vessel. Fortunately, *Dolaura*'s length made it stable enough for James to use the telescope to bird watch or to scope out and pick spots on shore for hunting.

The ship's interior was luxurious. *Dolaura*'s dining room measured 7.3 by 5.5 metres and had a fireplace for warmth and pale blue brocade-covered comfy chairs. Light glinted off the Spanish mahogany panelling on the walls. The dining room could comfortably seat twenty-four guests, with plenty of service room. The vessel was like a mansion,

VISITORS WHO SIGNED
THE YACHT'S GUESTBOOK
INCLUDED GERMANY'S
KAISER WILHELM II.

with a wet room, a library, a smoking room, and a special room for fishing tackle and guns. But the pièce de résistance was the Dunsmuir private stateroom that included a large sitting room, a bedroom, and a bathroom with marble wash basins and a bathtub of Doulton glazed ceramic.

There is an illuminating blue-covered guest book, where visitors to the *Dolaura* signed their names. The first guest to sign was Kaiser Wilhelm II of Germany in June 1908. James took his family to Europe to pick up the *Dolaura* and take a shakedown cruise of some European ports. The kaiser spotted the *Dolaura* after the Dunsmuir vessel had been through the Kiel Canal locks. He wrote to James, inviting him aboard his yacht, the *Hohenzollern*. James took the tour and then invited the kaiser aboard the *Dolaura*. The German emperor was impressed by his tour of the new ship (newer than his!).

Also notable in the guest book is the one-word signature "Norfolk." This was the gentleman, the fifteenth Earl of Norfolk, the Earl Marshal, whose signature appears on an invitation to the coronation of Edward VII sent to the Dunsmuirs. There is also a record here of the *Dolaura* being in Quebec City for that city's tercentenary (three hundredth anniversary). Some of the Dominion's leaders came aboard and signed the guest book: Shaughnessy, Grey, and Strathcona, to name a few. James sold the *Dolaura* before his death in 1920.

ROBERT HARVEY'S SABRETACHE *and* SPURS

ROBERT AND ELIZABETH HARVEY moved into Craigdarroch with their grandmother Joan because their parents had both died. They were two of the youngest children of Joan's second-eldest daughter, Agnes, who'd had a total of five children.

Robert Dunsmuir Harvey was only twelve years old when he came to live at Craigdarroch; he and his sister had been orphaned in 1889. Their parents had died of typhoid fever, their mother first in Nanaimo and their father a few months later in California, where he'd gone to recuperate.

Robert didn't have his third-floor room in the castle for long: His grandmother Joan sent him to Trinity College boarding school in Ontario just five months after the move. He later did well at the Royal Military College in Kingston (as exhibited by the trophies in his room).

Two months after graduating in 1899, Robert joined the Fourth (Queen's Own) Hussars, a British Army cavalry regiment. He quickly earned a promotion to lieutenant near the end of the following year. (Another lieutenant in this regiment was Winston Churchill.)

The Hussars were serving in India when Robert joined. It was a difficult assignment, and the regiment lost more than five hundred men to illness in just five years. In August 1901, Robert succumbed to liver disease at age twenty-three.

A WATERCOLOUR
AND GOUACHE
PAINTING OF
ROBERT DUNSMUIR
HARVEY, C. 1900

There is in the collection a magnificent watercolour painted around 1900 (not long before Robert died) in Secunderabad, India. It depicts Robert sitting on a horse in his elaborate Hussars uniform and pith helmet, with his sword and sabretache. Beneath the saddle is an animal skin, possibly an Indian leopard. The sabretache hangs from three golden cords and reaches the midpoint of the sword's length. The horse has a long red ornamental tassel hanging from the halter under its chin.

A sabretache is a kind of messenger bag with long straps, allowing cavalry officers to wear it athwart the body, if necessary. Gold-embroidered red felt is sewn onto a stiff leather-and-cardboard backing. These satchels often held military documents, and their owners were empowered to place regimental honours on

THE REGIMENTAL
SABRETACHE
WORN BY ROBERT
DUNSMUIR HARVEY

A PORTRAIT
OF ROBERT
DUNSMUIR
HARVEY

their sabretaches, even if they hadn't taken part in the campaign. Some of the campaigns noted on Robert's sabretache include Inkerman and Sevastopol from the Crimean War.

Adding to the suite of Robert's military effects in the Craigdarroch collection is a pair of dress spurs in a case. Manufactured by Maxwell & Company in London, the gilded cast metal arm that encircles the heel of a riding boot flags them as dress spurs.

To complete this set of military effects, the collection also has Robert's cartridge pouch. This item, for a cavalry officer to wear on his belt to hold ammunition, is made of leather with silver and a gilt brass version of the letters *VR*, the reigning monarch's royal cypher, with a crown atop it. Its hallmarks say it was made in Birmingham, England, in 1899

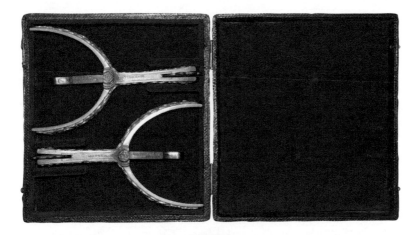

THE DRESS
SPURS WORN
BY ROBERT
DUNSMUIR
HARVEY

THE METAL
PART OF THE
CARTRIDGE
POUCH ROBERT
DUNSMUIR
HARVEY WORE
ON HIS BELT,
TO HOLD
AMMUNITION.

by Bent and Parker. The sterling silver backing panel behind the cypher has an intricately tooled border.

Robert spent time as a young boy in his room here at the castle, his parents gone but his sister nearby, finding himself wanting nothing but possibly feeling bereft. Mere months after he got here, he travelled east to a boys' boarding school where he knew no one and had no family nearby. Military college in Kingston and then the army was a logical progression, but a fellow who'd grown up in Nanaimo's temperate environment must have found the heat of India stifling. He died there of liver disease at the age of twenty-three. The regiment sent his effects to his sister and his grandmother in Victoria.

The sad story of Robert is just one of several poignant tales of Dunsmuir men and women in the military for Canada and for Great Britain. Many did their duty and many suffered. Here is a selection of their stories (a more comprehensive list is available in *Craigdarroch Military Hospital: A Canadian War Story*, published by the Craigdarroch Castle Historical Museum Society):

Maud Dunsmuir, the youngest of Joan's daughters, and her husband, Lieutenant-Colonel Reggie Chaplin, both served in the First World War. Having served with the Tenth Royal Hussars in the Boer War, he came out of retirement and worked with the British Remount Commission; he was based in Montreal. The commission found, purchased, and transported the horses needed for the war effort. Maud served with the Canadian Red Cross overseas, and their son, John Robert Chaplin, later served as aide-de-camp to Canada's twelfth Governor General, Julian Hedworth George Byng, first Viscount Byng of Vimy.

Joan's eldest son and the province's lieutenant governor from 1906 to 1909, James Dunsmuir was too old to fight in the First World War. His son, James Jr. (known as Boy in the family), wanted to see action as soon as possible. To expedite his trip to the front in Europe, Boy resigned his commission in the Canadian Mounted Rifles Battalion to join the Royal Scots Greys, a British cavalry regiment. He was on board the *Lusitania* from New York to London to join his new regiment when it was hit by a torpedo off the Irish coast on May 7, 1915. Boy was among the 1,193 passengers to perish. His father never recovered from losing his beloved son.

James Jr.'s sister and daughter of James and Laura Dunsmuir, Kathleen, served in the First World War providing a "motor kitchen," or canteen, for British troops in France. She organized, operated, and funded it, and it was where she met her husband. In the Second World War, Kathleen drove a mobile canteen in England. She was killed March 8, 1941, when London's Café de Paris was bombed. She had been celebrating her son's engagement.

Another of Joan's daughters, Mary Jean Dunsmuir Croft, raised money for the First World War effort on her own and also as a member of the Imperial Order Daughters of the Empire. She was honoured for her efforts.

Effie Dunsmuir's husband, the one she met in Dublin while visiting Jessie (and who later had Effie committed), was Vice-Admiral Somerset Arthur Gough-Calthorpe. He commanded the Royal Navy's Second Cruiser Squadron during the First World War. He was later commander-in-chief in the Mediterranean and high commissioner in Constantinople. He was named admiral of the fleet in 1925.

Another generation, another Harvey. Agnes's grandson, Robert Oliver Dunsmuir Harvey, lied about his age persuasively and joined the Gordon Highlanders in Victoria. He got sick with pneumonia while training at the Willows Fairground in Victoria, so they called his mother, Mabel Gaudin Harvey, who revealed his real age. He was (unhappily) released from service. He re-joined when he was of age, after enduring several "white feather" incidents, in which a stranger would ask why he wasn't in uniform. He never made it to Europe and went to law school after the war ended.

Guy Mortimer Audain was married to Sarah Byrd Dunsmuir (known as Byrdie in the family), Joan's granddaughter and daughter of her eldest son, James. Major Audain worked as liaison between the Indian and British armies. When he served in India before the war, he learned how to speak several Indian languages, including Hindi, Urdu, and Punjabi.

12

BEDROOM FURNITURE
MADE *for* JAMES DUNSMUIR

WITH THE OVERARCHING INFLUENCE Robert Dunsmuir and his family businesses had in Victoria—not least with the imposing profile of Craigdarroch Castle on the skyline—it's sometimes hard to remember that Robert and Joan's life (and the long-time influence of the Dunsmuir family) in BC really started in Nanaimo.

Consider Joan Dunsmuir arriving in BC. She and her husband landed in Departure Bay in 1851, after their six-month journey by sea from Scotland. (With no time-saving cut through the Panama Canal, the vessel *Pekin* had to travel "round the Horn" of South America and sail up the west coast of two continents to reach BC.) Robert had promised he'd build Joan a castle if she decided to come with him to BC. But when she saw the dirt floors of that first Hudson's Bay Company barracks housing in Fort Vancouver, where she gave birth to their first son, James, she probably wondered what she had done.

It wasn't as if their life in Scotland had been easy or luxurious. It hadn't been. The work was hard, and it had taken a lot of nerve to decide under pressure to come to BC in the short time they had to choose.

Still, for what she gave up in Scotland coming to BC, Joan and her family went from indentured employment with the Hudson's

Bay Company to being the richest family in British Columbia in less than three generations.

She had eight daughters and two sons. They all grew up as Victorian children did, with the boys following their father into the family business and the girls being trained in etiquette and languages, dance and needlepoint, and learning how to make a good marriage for the family.

Robert sent his younger son, Alex, to San Francisco to look after the family's coal and shipping interests there, and he sent his eldest son, James, to Wellington to oversee the mining operations. While James didn't last long as mine manager, he started a dynasty for the family with his wife, Laura Miller Surles Dunsmuir. He'd met Laura, a scion of southern US aristocracy, when he'd gone south to study mining engineering at his father's behest in the early 1870s. He'd become friends with Hannibal Surles and later met his sister. The family had been not-very-grand farmers before the Civil War and were pretty much the same after (although Laura encouraged the assumption she was a southern aristocrat from a family with huge land holdings, not a 120-hectare farm). Her father much preferred the scion of a BC mining family over another suitor, whose family means had been largely wiped out by the war.

So James Dunsmuir, twenty-four, married eighteen-year-old Laura Miller Surles a day after the American Fourth of July

While Laura did all right by marrying James, by 1919 her spurned suitor had parlayed $450 in savings into the largest selling cure for respiratory ailments in North America—Vicks VapoRub. Vicks was touted as an effective treatment during the 1918 flu pandemic; it had sales of more than $11 million in 1918.

• • •

holiday in 1875. They wed at the old Sardis Presbyterian Church in Cumberland Country, North Carolina. They then travelled to Vancouver Island to start their life together.

This bedroom suite was built in the United States around 1880 and shipped to James and Laura Dunsmuir's opulent home in Departure Bay, near Nanaimo, north of Victoria. The set consists of a bed (headboard, footboard, and side rails), a washstand, and a bureau.

It has a high headboard with a flat top, and a burled walnut panel is the central focus of the headboard. There's also a washstand with a removable marble top and a marble backsplash. In addition, the set contains a dressing table with a marble top and a mirror that pivots on metal pins from its frame.

There's a handwritten label that reads "James Dunsmuir, Departure Bay." It's known that James and Laura used the suite at their home in Departure Bay from 1880 or so until mid-1889. That's when they moved to Victoria, right around the time Robert

Dunsmuir died. Joan Dunsmuir was grieving the loss of her husband, so while she was waiting for Craigdarroch to be finished, she went travelling in Europe with her daughters. James and Laura moved into Fairview, the James Bay mansion where Joan and Robert had been living.

THE JAMES DUNSMUIR
BEDROOM SET

This suite might have been used by the couple at Fairview if Joan put her furnishings in storage. If not, then this went into storage. James and Laura completed their move in 1891.

The suite may have moved to Government House in Rockland in 1906 when James was tapped to be lieutenant-governor. He resigned early, in 1909. The family moved into the castle James had commissioned in 1910: Hatley Park in Esquimalt. The family used the bedroom set there until 1939, when it was sold while Laura's estate was being liquidated.

13

ELIZABETH HARVEY'S BOOK *of* COMMON PRAYER

ELIZABETH GEORGINA HARVEY was the daughter of Agnes Crooks Dunsmuir Harvey. Elizabeth and her younger brother, Robert, went to live with their formidable grandmother, at the castle built by their (late) formidable grandfather, after their parents died of typhoid fever.

Some people called her Lizzie. In the family, she was mostly known as Noël because of her birthday: Christmas Day. A prized possession became hers on another special Christmas, nine years after she'd moved into Craigdarroch, when her older brother James Swan Harvey and his wife, Mabel Gaudin Harvey, gave her a precious gift of prayer and song.

It's a small set of bound volumes in a leather case. One is the Book of Common Prayer, and the other, *Hymns, Ancient and Modern.* Each leather-bound volume has its title in gold on the front cover and on the spine of the book, as well. Each book fits comfortably in the palm of the hand, and they slide together into a leather case. You can almost feel the affection wrapped around this gift when you read the inscription, "Noël: With love from Mabel & Jim, Xmas 1899."

These books were a comfort to Elizabeth, always accompanying her to Sunday services in Victoria.

VICTORIA IS A RELIGIOUS CAPITAL, as were most places in Canada in the 1800s. The major faith divisions tended to be among Catholic, Protestant, and Jewish. (Victoria is home to Congregation Emanu-El, the oldest synagogue edifice still in use as a synagogue in Canada.)

There were further delineations among the Protestant faith in the family. Some of the Dunsmuirs went to the Anglican Christ Church Cathedral, and several of the daughters were married there. Robert and Joan went to St. Andrew's Presbyterian on the corner of Courtney Street and Gordon.

When Joan's daughter Jessie Sophia Dunsmuir married Sir Richard Musgrave in 1891, the wedding reportage in the *Colonist* newspaper of September 24, 1891 called it "the most fashionable and brilliant wedding witnessed in Victoria for many months."

Left:

THE PRAYER BOOK AND HYMNAL GIVEN TO "NOËL" DUNSMUIR FOR CHRISTMAS 1899

Right:

THE INSCRIPTION IN THE PRAYER BOOK GIVEN TO "NOËL" DUNSMUIR

The paper described the scene outside Christ Church Cathedral as the bride and her wedding party arrived. "Two o'clock was the hour set for the ceremony and at that time the body of the Cathedral was filled with invited guests while hundreds of ladies and dozens of gentlemen, not so highly honoured, crowded the side seats in the church, the aisles, the churchyard and the streets. Those fortunate in securing outside standing room were forced to content themselves with one short look at the bride as she entered the church."

And on the decorations: "Many a time has the old cathedral been decked with bright flowers for some festive event, but never more artistically or more effectively than yesterday. Palms predominated the decorations forming a wall of green between the chancel screen and the interested congregation. The choir rails were hidden in a wealth of white roses, asters, and verbena; the pulpit was festooned with ivy, relieved with hydrangea, and the alter was embedded in roses."

Even if you were standing outside the church, imagine the fragrance that would pour out once the doors were opened.

While it wasn't the current Christ Church Cathedral building where Jessie was married (the location of her wedding was in the second wooden cathedral built for the congregation on the spot where the Victoria law courts are now), the building of the current stone cathedral, which didn't happen until after the First World War, was helped by a $100,000 contribution from Laura, Mrs. James Dunsmuir.

Other Dunsmuir daughters and granddaughters were married in Christ Church Cathedral, including James Dunsmuir's youngest daughter Dola Frances, who married the naval officer Lieutenant Commander Henry James Francis Cavendish in August 1928; her marriage to "Dish" lasted until 1934.

AS NOTED, Joan and Robert belonged to St. Andrew's Presbyterian Church, as they had in Scotland. But it wasn't always an easy relationship.

Imagine you're Elizabeth Hamilton Dunsmuir, first daughter of Robert and Joan Dunsmuir. Born eight days after your parents were married in Scotland, you always had some sense of the scandal attached to your arrival, even after your family moved to another continent. Your parents were banned from their Presbyterian parish in Ayrshire until they confessed to their sin of "antenuptial fornication" and did penance; they were chastised and shunned for a while before being readmitted. All this within three years; they, along with you and your sister Agnes, departed Scotland for something new in North America. You were along for the epic six-month-long voyage between Scotland and British Columbia (around Cape Horn), and your brother James was born shortly after your arrival.

Robert and Joan started their lives in BC up island, closer to Nanaimo. The Presbyterian church there was also St. Andrew's, and the congregation met in the courthouse until they constructed a building in 1866 on Fitzwilliam Street. Robert Dunsmuir's name was listed on the Presbyterian communion roll when nineteen of the six hundred or so people living in Nanaimo called themselves Presbyterian.

Later, Robert and Joan Dunsmuir were among the first couples to become members of St. Andrew's Presbyterian Church in Victoria, but they reportedly didn't attend with any regularity. After Robert died, the family donated the large stained glass rose window (as well as two other windows) in his memory. Robert was buried from St. Andrew's in April 1889 and interred in Ross Bay Cemetery. As noted in Terry Reksten's book *The Dunsmuir Saga*, some twelve thousand people lined the route of his funeral procession between the family's pre-Craigdarroch mansion, Fairview, on Menzies Street near Quebec Street, to St. Andrew's Church and then to the cemetery.

14

PIERRE BERTON'S CARVED INITIALS

PIERRE BERTON may well be the Victoria College student whose name is most familiar to people from coast to coast to coast. The journalist, historian, and television personality carved his name into the crown moulding of the common room at Victoria College when it was in Craigdarroch Castle, as did several others. While Berton ended up graduating from the University of British Columbia, his formative college years were spent at Victoria College.

Berton was born in Whitehorse, Yukon, in 1920, and his family moved to Dawson City the next year. His father had moved to Yukon for the Klondike gold rush, and his mother had moved from Toronto to Yukon to teach kindergarten. The family moved to Victoria when Pierre was twelve, the same year he became a Boy Scout. He credits the Scouts with keeping him from a life of petty crime. As he noted in a story for the *Toronto Star* titled "My Love Affair with the Scout Movement", he wrote his first stories while a Scout and later said, "The first newspaper I was ever associated with was a typewritten publication issued by the Seagull Patrol of St. Mary's Troop."

When he got to Victoria College, he joined the school paper, the *Microscope* (the *Mike*), as a cartoonist. In one serial, *The Curse of the College*, the trench-coated sleuth Gridley Quayle sought the "Fiend of Craigdarroch."

He was there for two years; only in his second year did he find his footing, exchanging chemistry for history, and his grades started to improve. He went to the University of British Columbia in Vancouver for his final two years and worked at the student paper there, the *Ubyssey*, while completing a history degree. The *Ubyssey* provided an experience that launched many Canadian journalists, and Berton was no exception. He also worked summers in the mining camps up north in the Klondike to pay for school.

Berton was able to get hands-on newspaper experience at a young age, as so many staff had been sent overseas in the Second World War. He found himself in the army in 1942 and sought to be trained as an officer. Berton wanted to get overseas, but, as he wrote in *Starting Out 1920–1945* (McClelland & Stewart, 1987), when he finally did get over in March 1945, he was told he would have to test again to be an intelligence officer, as the Canadian and British courses were so different. By the time he'd done that, the war was over.

In 1947, Berton found himself in Toronto. Soon after, he became editor at *Maclean's* magazine. Ten years later, he was working on CBC Television's current affairs show *Close-Up* and also as a panellist on the popular game show *Front Page Challenge*. Berton wrote his first book in 1953 about the Royal Family, and he went on to write almost a book a year, mostly popular Canadian history, until 2004.

The great gift Berton gave Canadians was their own history, told in a way that made it engrossing. He wrote about the Klondike, the building of the Canadian Pacific Railway, the Dionne quintuplets, Vimy Ridge, the Depression, the gold rush, and the depiction of Canada and Canadians in Hollywood films, to name but a few.

He also wrote history for young readers, particularly about the War of 1812, the North, Canada's West, and the gold rush.

"Without Pierre Berton there would scarcely be any Canadian history left. . . . For . . . years he has popularized Canadian history in a way that nobody else was doing," said the historian J.L. Granatstein, quoted by Sandra Martin in the *Globe and Mail*, December 1, 2004.

Additional Victoria College graduates include the artists Bill Reid and Jack Shadbolt and the scientist Frances Kelsey. Dr. Kelsey was a pharmacologist who studied at McGill University in Montreal and moved to Chicago to do her PhD. Later, as a reviewer for the US Food and Drug Administration, she was able to prevent the release of the anti-nausea/sleep aid drug thalidomide to the American marketplace. Her action in preventing the drug's use in the United States precluded the congenital deformities and the heartache thalidomide caused thousands of people in Canada and overseas. In 1962, President John F. Kennedy presented Dr. Kelsey with the President's Award for Distinguished Federal Civilian Service; she was only the second woman to ever receive the honour.

SO YOU'RE A BORED YOUNG MAN, aged about seventeen. You're sitting in a stuffy, hot room for a history lecture that bores you because it's from too long ago. You know you're in a room soaked with Dunsmuir history and Great War meaning; you think, *Why aren't we talking about that?* Next, you're off to a class in what used to be the Dunsmuir billiard room, once used by the city's wealthiest families, including the young women, as Queen Victoria had made billiards more than a little bit all right—that room is where you study physics and chemistry. The top-floor dance hall, used by aristocracy and those in the merchant marine and military who wished they were, has a corner that serves as your library (see page 114).

Later, you're in the Dunsmuir drawing room (where you're sitting for the history lecture, and later the English and French lessons) with original architectural details, such as one of seventeen fireplaces, behind the chalkboard. The classics are studied in the one-time kitchen, and social events, as well as math classes, are held in the dining room. The Victoria College common room is on the second floor, where Joan Dunsmuir's sitting room used to be. That's where you sneak off for a nap!

The feeling of going to school in a mansion or a castle might remind some of boys' boarding school stories of old, from *Tom Brown's School Days* to *Chums* to *Boy's Own* almanacs, even though most students lived in Victoria and traipsed into Victoria College daily.

These are sketches of life at Victoria College, which inhabited Craigdarroch Castle between 1921 and 1946. The college was an offshoot of McGill University, which granted its degrees initially. It started with fewer than 250 students and ballooned to more than 600 by 1946.

Dangerous overcrowding following increased enrolment after the Second World War and fire danger were the issues that finally saw Victoria College vacate Craigdarroch and move to the former Normal School building at Lansdowne and Foul Bay Roads, now a campus of Camosun College. Victoria College became the University of Victoria in 1963 and moved to its own campus farther up the peninsula.

15

RADIATOR
BRUSHES

MAGINE YOU ARE A YOUNG WOMAN, born into the poorer class
in Victorian-era Victoria, or you moved to the capital from back
east or from England, hearing there was lots of domestic work.
You already have a job in service, but there's a fellow where you
work who's a bit handsy and you'd like to move on. You see an ad
in the *Colonist* (you can read, thanks to the Sisters of St. Ann):
"Wanted: Experienced parlour maid. Apply between the hours of
1 and 2 or 5 and 8. Mrs. Dunsmuir, Craigdarroch."

You get the electric railway along Fort Street and get off just
before the big gates. You're hot in your best Sunday outfit and
hat (tidy looking, but not appearing as though you're putting on
airs). You want to take your time walking up that hill from the
gate (clever you: you left lots of time, as you didn't want to arrive
all hot and in a bother) and find your way to the kitchen entrance.

You almost lose your nerve on that walk when you see the view
from the top of the hill and the expanse of the estate. But you carry
on, ring the bell at the kitchen door, and introduce yourself, saying
you're here about the job.

A girl even younger than you, wearing a shy smile and a uniform still fragrant with pressing by a hot iron, lets you into the
house and introduces you to the housekeeper. This older woman is
a bit terse and unsmiling; she doesn't look you in the eye but says,

"I think you'll do fine, my girl." Then she says, "The lady of the house will want to meet you. Just wait here."

The lady of the house! That must mean Mrs. Joan Dunsmuir herself. You never thought you'd get to meet Mrs. Dunsmuir, even though you'd seen her from a distance at church sometimes.

You stand when Mrs. Joan Dunsmuir enters the room. She's a petite woman, but you can sense the size and certain resolve of her personality. She looks you up and down, instructs you to turn around once, and asks where your people are from and when you saw them last.

"You may go" are her final words to you. Having been dismissed, you look for the way out with tears burning behind your eyes.

As you scuttle toward the door where you entered, Molly (for that was the name of the young woman who'd opened the door for you), breathless, catches up with you. Smiling, she says, "Where are you going? They want you. You're hired. Come with me. I'll show you your room."

THERE ARE CURRENTLY TWO ROOMS in the castle that were live-in servants' quarters, located on the third floor going down (there were others during the Dunsmuir era). They are small but comfortable and attractively decorated. It was difficult to hire servants in the mid-nineteenth century in Victoria, and even harder to keep them, so employers did everything they could. Joan Dunsmuir paid her servants reasonably well, and she rewarded loyalty. In her will, the first two people mentioned were servants, Annie Ruth and Ellen. If they were still working at Joan's house when she died, her will promised each $500.

Having servants in Victorian Victoria was both a signalling of wealth and class and a necessity. Few gentlewomen of the day knew much of what it took to run a household, beyond what was needed to instruct servants, "and were often overwhelmed by

Facing page:

THIS POSTER
FROM MRS. LINLEY
SAMBOURNE'S
1910 NOTEBOOK
SHOWS HOW
HARD DOMESTIC
WORK WAS.

the unaccustomed drudgery," says Lorraine Brown, in her 2007 history MA thesis titled *Domestic Service in British Columbia, 1850–1914*.

It certainly wasn't easy work. In *Henry & Self: The Private Life of Sarah Crease*, author Kathryn Bridge lists the typical duties of a female homemaker. "When they were not giving birth or raising children, colonial women were responsible for: the physical maintenance of the house and furnishings, the cleaning and upkeep of personal items such as clothing, linen and bedding; the acquisition, processing, storage and preparation of food. . . . They also mended, sewed, grew and harvested crops" (p. 246).

A small poster for sale in the castle gift shop (see page 97) lists a maid's duties. While there is no documentation of what Mrs. Dunsmuir expected of her servants, the 1891 federal census says Mrs. Dunsmuir had an average of six employees in service (three living in the house and three more day workers). This list is from Mrs. Linley Sambourne's notebook of 1910, a British document of the same era.

THE PREFERENCE OF BC EMPLOYERS of the day was for domestic servants who were white, sometimes locals but more often brought over from England. Indigenous people had little interest in being part of a servant class to settlers. Later, Chinese immigrants (mostly men) undertook some domestic service duties.

Lorraine Brown noted in her research about domestic service in BC that "while class distinctions did exist, British Columbia's white domestic servants were more independent than their British counterparts. They were usually employed in one-servant households, often of necessity working with their mistresses on a familiar basis. In an understocked market, they could also change employers frequently." (*Domestic Service in British Columbia, 1850–1914* by Lorraine Brown, 1995 MA thesis)

MAID'S DUTIES

The 1891 Federal Census reported that Mrs. Robert Dunsmuir of Craigdarroch hired an average number of six household employees. Those stated to be living in the house (or onsite) were: Kate McDonald (maid) native of Ontario, age 24; Ester Smith (maid) native of England age 19; and Isaac Nash (groom).

A housemaid's daily chores were formidable. While no records remain documenting a Craigdarroch housemaid's chores, the following description taken from Mrs. Linley Sambourne's* notebook reveals much:

7:00 a.m.	Bring my hot drinking water, sweep down and thoroughly wash stairs and make bathroom ready, and lavatory. Own breakfast.
8:00 a.m.	Bring my hot water. Draw up blinds and empty and take away bath - always use basin cloth, and wipe tumblers.
8:30 a.m.	Clean grate in drawing room, and thoroughly dust and sweep room, wipe round parquet floor. Clean all brass. Open windows front and back. Water and wipe with wet cloth plants and water window plants.
9:30 a.m.	Open beds and turn over mattresses to air, all windows opened. Take away slops, always remembering to have slop cloth clean. Wash thoroughly washstands. See water bottles filled - glasses clean, marble clean etc. and taps only rubbed with a leather after well wiping. Bed made. Mr. Roy's room finished by 10 a.m., rugs and chairs brushed - floor wiped with damp cloth. Furniture dusted and handles well rubbed with a leather. Silver things put in drawer after wiping with leather.
10:30 a.m.	My bedroom thoroughly brushed and wiped round, shaking duster outside window, brass rubbed, wardrobe dusted inside and out. Dressing table brushed and dusted and silver rubbed with leather - put my boots, hat and coat, gloves and wrap ready for me on the sofa.
11:00 a.m.	Lunch. Prepare room for special cleaning. Have dust sheets, and long broom ready.
1:00 p.m.	Answer hall bell until 20 past while House parlour maid dresses. Hot water jug filled in mine and spare room, basins wiped. My bed arranged for resting.
2:00 p.m.	Maid's dinner.
2:30 p.m.	Look through bedrooms and take away any soiled boots. Finish room for special cleaning and wash upper landing.
4:30 p.m.	Tea.
5:00 p.m.	Look through my drawers and take away things needing mending.
6:00 p.m.	Hot water for bedrooms. Blinds pulled down at dusk and windows locked. Put out dress for dinner.
7:00 p.m.	Tidy drawing room - put cushions tidy and papers, dust tables and piano. See to lights and fires swept.
8:00 p.m.	Assist and wait at table and after see to bedrooms, turn down beds - wash stands wiped. Hot water. Chambers etc.
9:00 p.m.	Supper.
10:00 p.m.	Bed.

* Taken from Mrs. Linley Sambourne's notebook (1910)
LINLEY SAMBOURNE HOUSE, 18 STAFFORD TERRACE, LONDON W8

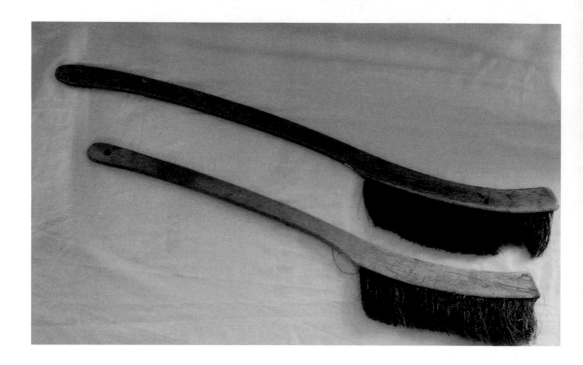

THESE BRUSHES WERE USED TO CLEAN BETWEEN THE "PLEATS" OF A RADIATOR, AND THE DUST THEY DISLODGED WAS THEN SWEPT UP AND DISCARDED.

Literature shows an unfortunate pattern for employers that saw them engage young English women as servants, only to have the young woman immigrate, work in service for a while, and then marry and set up her own household.

In her research on domestic service in BC between the mid-1800s and the start of the First World War, Brown quoted an editorial in an 1861 edition of the *British Colonist* (probably seen in England) that noted one of the advantages of immigration: "No sooner does an unmarried woman arrive here than a host of admirers offer to make her happy for life. . . . We have at least a thousand young men willing to get married, the scarcity of unmarried females is an inducement for parents having large families to make this town their home." ("Inducements to Families to Settle in Victoria," *British Colonist*. Victoria, November 30, 1861)

If you ever lived in a house with hot-water radiators, you may have experienced a modern-day version of these radiator brushes, believed to be original to the castle. Servants used them to clean between the radiator fin sections, to dislodge any dust and debris that would then be swept up and discarded.

Craigdarroch was heated with radiators right from the start, in addition to the fireplaces that provided some heat but more atmosphere. (The castle had all the modern conveniences of the day: hot and cold running water, as well as gas *and* electric lights.)

Radiators create consistent warmth because water heated in a boiler by coal or gas is pumped through a pipe and through the metal (usually cast iron) accordion-like "pleats" of the radiator. The water drains through another pipe and returns to the boiler to be reheated. Victorian-era metal radiators were often finished with elaborately designed scrollwork, executed by top-end designers and artisan metalworkers.

16

SPEAKING
TUBE

A VISITOR TO CRAIGDARROCH CASTLE for an event needs to use the restroom and seems to remember seeing one on the second floor (the functioning restroom is in the visitors' centre; the one on the second floor is an exhibit). Something catches the visitor's eye that they've never seen before: it looks like a little metal funnel sticking out from the wall on the second floor between Jessie's room and what would have been the guest bedroom, where Joan's younger son, Alex Dunsmuir, stayed when he visited from San Francisco. It's made of cast brass, and it's a speaking tube. It was the latest communication technology in 1890, a kind of intercom using two cones and an air pipe that allowed people in various parts of the house to communicate.

A speaking tube, a nineteenth-century intercom, works similarly to two tin cans and some string, or to naval communications systems. It involves a cone at one end for the speaker and the same at the other end for the listener, connected by a tube. Operated with push buttons, speaking tubes modernized the system of bells often used in nineteenth-century houses to summon servants.

Those bells were often on springs and connected to bell pulls of one kind or another, linking rooms in the main house to servants' quarters. The use of battery power morphed bells into buzzers, and before long, speaking tubes were in vogue. Their major drawback was lack of privacy, and as we moved into the twentieth century,

A SPEAKING TUBE, SHOWN HERE ABOVE A MORE MODERN SWITCH IN A CRAIGDARROCH HALLWAY.

A SPEAKING TUBE WAS
CONSIDERED HIGH-TECH
IN ITS DAY.

internal telephone and buzzer systems prevailed. Speaking tubes are still used in some contexts such as playground equipment, because they are low cost and low tech, not requiring power.

The speaking-tube hardware is from a company in New Britain, Connecticut, and the pattern of the speaking tube is called "colonial" (it was the primary pattern used throughout the castle on domestic hardware such as speaking tubes and light-switch plates).

The two rooms near the speaking tube speak volumes, but each holds a different story. One room was Jessie Dunsmuir's, and the other was used by her brother Alex when he was in Victoria. Alex was thirteen years older than Jessie and had lived in San Francisco for a while. Jessie probably knew Alex had a problem with drink, and she also probably knew something she shouldn't have: her brother Alex was living in sin (as her mother might have put it) with a woman in San Francisco named Josephine Wallace. On paper, Josephine was Alex's landlady, but she had been known to introduce herself as Mrs. Alex Dunsmuir.

Joan and Robert (before he died) were absolutely opposed to any marital union of Alex and his paramour because Josephine was a divorcee with a daughter. Alex had largely raised that daughter, Edna, as his own, and she went on to be a star of stage and screen as Edna Hopper, after marrying the actor DeWolf Hopper. Alex had to live a double life, and that might be why he drank. As was revealed later, he was an obnoxious drunk and clearly an addict with a disease that led to dementia and an early death. Sometimes, when he came to Victoria to visit, he would stay at Craigdarroch, but other times he would stay at the Union Club so he could drink.

Robert died unexpectedly in 1889 and, just as unexpectedly, left everything to his wife, Joan. The sons, James and Alex, had worked all their adult lives in the family coal business and had expected to control it after their father died. They didn't, and their mother wouldn't relinquish control; she was looking out for a number of unmarried daughters whom she wanted to be sure she could help make good marriages. One of these daughters was Jessie.

Jessie Sophia was the third-youngest Dunsmuir. She was twenty-four and approaching spinsterhood when she moved into Craigdarroch in September 1890 with her mother, sisters, and orphaned niece and nephew. The implicit plan to use the wealth-signalling flamboyance of the castle as suitable mate bait worked: Jessie was married to the Irish baronet Sir Richard Musgrave by September 1891 and so was the first Dunsmuir to rate an entry in *Debrett's Peerage*. The wedding itself at Christ Church Cathedral was larger than life. As many as thirty attendants (bridesmaids and flower girls) preceded Jessie down the aisle. Some three hundred guests were invited to the reception at Craigdarroch.

Jessie moved with her new husband to his 3,200-hectare estate in County Waterford (which Dunsmuir money helped improve), but she found life in Ireland lonesome. Being Lady Musgrave gave her access to the Court of St. James's in London, the social machinations of Irish aristocracy, and the social events replete with young, unmarried military officers. She needed only to get her unmarried sisters in the same room.

17

FIRE SCREENS

A FIRESCREEN WAS MEANT TO PROTECT PEOPLE NEAR THE FIREPLACE FROM GETTING TOO HOT OR TO HIDE THE FIREBOX WHEN NOT IN USE.

VISITORS TO CRAIGDARROCH for an event during the winter (when the Dunsmuirs lived here and even during later eras) would soon learn where the drafts were, as well as the pools of warmth, and position themselves accordingly to stay comfortable.

Every room at Craigdarroch seems to have at least one fireplace; some areas, such as the drawing room, have two.

The castle is a big place to keep warm; the high ceilings and the way heat rises made it hard to make a room cozy. A fireplace always helps—if you're close by. But the downside of proximity can be overheating, flushed cheeks, and feeling sweaty and faint.

For those who struggle to get a roaring fire rolling from a combo of tinder, kindling, logs, and a puff of air, it can be hard to believe there is a specific piece of nineteenth-century furniture designed to protect room occupants from overheating because of a fire that is burning hot, or from burns, should sparks fly from the fire.

It's called a fireplace screen. It is also used to cover a fireplace cavity (or firebox) when there is no fire burning, for aesthetic appeal.

The fire screen has several designs. The most familiar one might be the rectangle on the longer edge, mounted on two sets of feet (a set at either end). This is known as the cheval or horse screen. Another is a smaller screen, of various shapes and sizes, positioned on a pole stabilized by a tripod footing. This design allows the screen to be positioned at various points on the pole, so that a person's face can be shielded from the heat no matter how they are seated in relation to the fireplace. A third fire screen consists of three panels, one bigger panel facing out toward the room with two smaller panels angled toward the rear like wings, providing some stability. This style covers the fireplace cavity well.

The fireplace screens at Craigdarroch fall into the cheval and pole styles. One fire screen in the drawing room, with a rosewood frame and featuring an elaborate embroidered image of a male peacock (display in repose), is a pole-style screen. Another featured in the drawing room is of the cheval style, featuring a carved rosewood frame with feet, encasing an embroidered fabric panel. This fire screen could be a Craigdarroch Castle original, but there is insufficient provenance documentation to be certain.

Fire screens were also useful in stopping the drafts that could emanate from a fireplace chimney flue when it was not in use. The bigger screens were best for this, and the example in the billiard room features a hawk design of Berlin wool work. Berlin wool work is similar to needlepoint but is executed with wool yarn (rather than silk) on a canvas base. Advances in fabric dyes in the mid-1800s made bright colours possible, and they offered the impression of three dimensions with finessed shading of colour in the work.

The castle has never depended entirely on fireplaces for heat. In photos taken when Craigdarroch housed Victoria College, big hot-water radiators are visible on either side of the fireplace on the far wall. More and more of these appeared in various rooms as the fireplaces fell into disuse. But the radiator in the corner of the Garden Entrance is an original fixture, still fully functional. While hot-water radiators such as the castle's had been patented in 1874, they were still somewhat of a novelty when they were installed in the castle when it was built in the late 1880s. The fuel for heating the water at Craigdarroch was originally coal; later it was heating oil.

18

CRAIGDARROCH
MILITARY HOSPITAL,
SEPTEMBER 25, 1919

MAGINE YOU ARE A YOUNG MAN, one of the 450,000 who have
served your country overseas in the Great War. At last, one day,
you are one of the more than 70,000 Canadians returning home with
injuries or permanent disabilities as a result of your war service.

En route home, on the quay in Le Havre, France, a smiling young
woman with wavy blond hair hands you a slice of buttered bread and
a hard-boiled egg. The gift of her smile and the touch of her hand are
almost as welcome as the food. This young woman was Kathleen
Euphemia Dunsmuir, second-youngest daughter of James Dunsmuir,
one-time premier and lieutenant governor of BC, and his wife, Laura.

When the war had started in 1914, "Kat" had been content help-
ing to raise money in Victoria by presenting (and performing in) benefit concerts. But she was desperate to be more hands-on. Early 1915
found her overseas, working at the Le Havre canteen with a friend,
exhausted and loving it. She didn't hesitate to write home, entreating
family for the money to provide comfort to others: "How they do love
on a cold morning at 5 or 6 o'clock to have hot chocolate and buns!"
(The work of Kat and her friends was noted in the *Daily Colonist*
newspaper in Victoria on April 22, 25, May 7, and October 16, 1915.)

It was in Le Havre that Kat met her husband, Major Arthur Selden
Humphreys, assistant quartermaster general. Their marriage meant
Kat had to return to England for the duration of the war, as the wives
of officers serving in France weren't allowed to remain there.

The couple returned to Victoria after the war, and Humphreys was aide-de-camp to Lieutenant-Governor Walter Nichol. The couple had four children, but by 1930 things had soured. Humphreys went to Shanghai, and Kathleen went to Hollywood. She had always wanted a show-business career, and while she was no longer a true ingenue starlet, she was Dunsmuir wealthy. Any meetings she "took" tended to have an implicit transactional subtext: she would bankroll a production in return for a starring role.

Oddly, this worked out for Kathleen only when she returned to Victoria in the late 1920s, when the British film business was operating with a quota system (much like the modern-day Canadian point system used to attract government film subsidies). Kathleen worked with a sketchy British film production house, Commonwealth Productions, to shoot a film at Hatley Castle. That was shelved for another called *The Crimson Paradise*, in which Kathleen was a star. It was a convoluted picture: prizefighter-biopic-cum-story-of-man-transformed-by-love-and-nature.

"Canada's first all-talking motion picture" (*Embattled Shadows: A History of Canadian Cinema 1895–1939* by Peter Morris, MQUP) enjoyed a late-night premiere in Victoria and a three-day run before mercifully sinking into obscurity.

Commonwealth Productions couldn't pay its bills, so Kathleen ended up $50,000 in the hole. She was able to get additional help from her mother and resumed a version of her previous lifestyle. After her mother died in 1937, Kathleen went to Europe. It wasn't long before there was another war and Kat was back in London helping out at the British Columbia House canteen on Regent Street.

Her son, Jim, was in the Royal Air Force. Her eldest daughter worked with her at the canteen and her younger daughter couldn't wait to do the same. When Jim said he was getting married, Kathleen thought the Café de Paris in London would be the perfect location. That's where they were March 8, 1941, when a bomb hit the underground restaurant's air vent. Jim and his new bride were injured in the explosion; Kathleen was killed.

YOU'RE A YOUNG SOLDIER on your way home from the carnage in Europe. When a nice lady hands you a snack, you have no way of knowing you will be recuperating in her grandmother's house in Victoria. You are sent to the Home for Repatriated Soldiers of the Great War in what used to be the residence of the Dunsmuir family, Craigdarroch Castle. Renovations are extensive: hospital accommodations for up to sixty patients, hot water for steam heating and therapeutic baths, plumbing for institutional bath and toilet rooms, and a dumbwaiter for getting meals from the main kitchen to the new "diet kitchens" and the men on the wards.

You are there on September 25, 1919, when His Royal Highness the Prince of Wales arrives to open the facility; people are crowded on the grounds, verandas, and balconies, hoping for a glimpse of the man who would become Edward VIII (see page 110 for castle photo). He speaks to you and others when he walks through your ward. He pays particular attention to soldiers who are in bed and

ROYALTY CAME TO THE CASTLE IN 1919 TO OPEN THE CRAIGDARROCH MILITARY HOSPITAL.

HRH PRINCE OF
WALES ENTERS
CRAIGDARROCH,
SEPTEMBER 25,
1919. HE IS AT THE
TOP OF THE STAIRS,
WEARING A NAVAL
OFFICER'S HAT WITH
A WHITE TOP.

questions men wearing medals or ribbons signalling service in South Africa. Had he asked you, you might tell him your heart's desire is just to get better, stronger, healthy enough to head home from the castle and reclaim your pre-war life.

Before departing, His Royal Highness made the trip to the tower and had a chance to view the stupendous vista from Craigdarroch's highest point: the Strait of Juan de Fuca and the mountains on the American Olympic Peninsula and, from another vantage point, Mount Douglas and Mount Tolmie looking north to the Saanich Peninsula.

Craigdarroch Castle had been sussed out early on as a possible location for a military hospital. Its owner, Solomon Cameron, had won it in a raffle in 1910. It was empty, and the Bank of Montreal had assumed control, as Mr. Cameron was overextended.

Time was of the essence, as the first troops to be "invalided" out had already landed in Halifax. Craigdarroch was officially taken over by the Department of Soldiers' Civil Re-establishment (DSCR) on January 29, 1919. It was September before the castle resembled a hospital more than it did a house. Each floor had a nurses' "sitting room," linen storage, a diet kitchen, and a serving room "fitted with appliances for keeping the food warm after it [had] been sent up" via dumbwaiter from the remodelled central kitchen on the main floor, as noted in chapter 2:1, p. 48 of *Craigdarroch Military History: A Canadian War Story*. The hospital kitchen was one large room, with a large range, a food preparation table, a steam table, and racks with several shelves.

CORNER OF THE REMODELLED KITCHEN

—Photo by R. L. Pea ck

The culinary arrangements at Craigdarroch Hospital have not been slighted. In addition to the big main kitchen on the main floor, there will be a smaller diet kitchen on each of the upper floors, in order that bed cases may receive the best of attention. A dumb-waiter also connects the main pantry with the serving-room on each floor. Miss H. Hansford is the dietitian. Off the kitchen is a sunny, glass-enclosed space which will be reserved for the maids.

THE KITCHEN IN THE CRAIGDARROCH MILITARY HOSPITAL

The second floor, which had originally housed Joan's bedroom, bathroom, and closet, underwent enormous changes. The entire floor of one portion was raised to accommodate plumbing pipes, making possible the installation of two shower stalls, a bathtub room, four toilet stalls, four wash basins, and two dental basins. These fixtures are still there as part of the exhibited collection. The third floor saw another institutional bathroom installed, which eliminated the original Dunsmuir bathroom (a version of the latter has been re-created).

The billiard room, and bedrooms were used to house soldiers. The basement housed the plumbing for all the new washrooms as well as for the hydrotherapy used to help the young soldiers. Many suffered from what was called "shell shock," which we now call post-traumatic stress disorder. Shell shock didn't inspire sympathy from some military doctors. Sir Andrew Macphail noted in his book *Official History of the Canadian Forces in the Great War,*

1914–1919: The Medical Services, Ottawa, Ministry of National Defense, 1925: "Shell-shock is a manifestation of childishness and femininity. Against such there is no remedy." The use of the term as a diagnosis started to fade when medical personnel offered alternatives: battle neurosis, functional disability, or NYDN (not yet diagnosed, nervous).

The approaches to treatment were basic: rest, good food, and exercise. Games were encouraged, and the recovering men were able to play tennis on the castle's south lawn. Beyond that, women known as ward aides helped determine the needs of the recovering men when it came to mental stimulation and therapy.

Some of the men were sent elsewhere to learn a new occupation, such as working as an electrician, boat building, motor repair, shoe repair, carpentry, cabinetmaking, gardening, or raising poultry. Hospital ward occupations were meant to lead less to a new job than to a greater sense of well-being, physical strengthening, and self-esteem. These softer skills bestowed by craftwork, such as painting, weaving, or basketry, could even be acquired while still bedridden.

This is where the ward aides came in.

As Walter Segsworth, the Director of Vocational Training, noted in his book, *Retraining Canada's Disabled Soldiers*, Taché, Printer to the King's Most Excellent Majesty, Ottawa, 1920:

> It has been proven without a doubt that properly trained girls are the only ones who are uniformly successful in introducing the idea of work and bringing about the first mental stimulus at the bedside. . . . Before the ward aide work was introduced the men in the wards were idle.
>
> Walter E. Segsworth
> Director of Vocational Training, DSCR

This kind of work is believed to have been early days for the field now known as occupational therapy.

19

DANCE CARDS

I T IS A LARGE ROOM, with a beautiful, shiny, wooden floor—perfect for dancing. There are several alcoves where musicians might position themselves. The ceiling angles down in places, toward the windows, and there are chairs positioned along the walls for those who prefer to sip punch or catch their breath after a whirl through the lancers (a dance done by couples in formation, an ancestor of square dancing). Or a chair might contain—heaven forbid—a seated wallflower, a young lady who didn't have all the slots on her dance card claimed before the party got underway.

ONE CORNER OF
THE FOURTH FLOOR
DANCE HALL

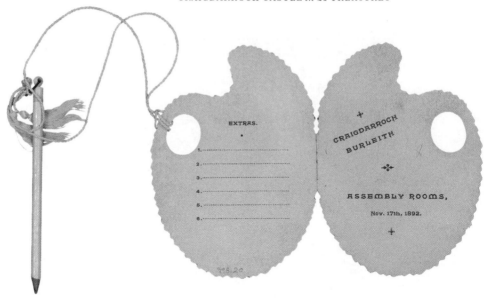

EXTRAS.

1.
2.
3.
4.
5.
6.

CRAIGDARROCH
BURLEITH

ASSEMBLY ROOMS,
Nov. 17th, 1892.

THE DANCE CARD COVER NOTED THE DATE OF THE EVENT.

The views are stupendous from the windows high up in Craig-darroch Castle: the Olympic Mountains across the Strait of Juan de Fuca in the United States, as well as looking away from the water and toward the growing city of Victoria. But it is night-time, and the view inside the room beats the outside view of stars and darkness.

There are women both beautiful and plain, young and not. All are dressed in their best, possibly a boned bodice in a luxurious brocade fabric or a jewel-toned velvet with ruffles, and a skirt with a bustle or a train. Most will have their hair upswept and pinned, with curls or ringlets escaping to soften any severe lines around the face. The gentlemen would be resplendent in tails, or the military men in dress uniform.

The chandeliers might be hissing with dancing gaslight, which, along with all the dancing bodies, serves to make the room warm. There would be flowers, maybe bunting on the walls, portraits of royalty—and perhaps of Joan and (the late) Robert Dunsmuir.

The dance hall on the fourth floor of Craigdarroch was the scene for many an elaborate event whose focus was music and dancing (and drinking and eating). To keep an evening's terpsicho-rean commitments straight, a lady had a dance card.

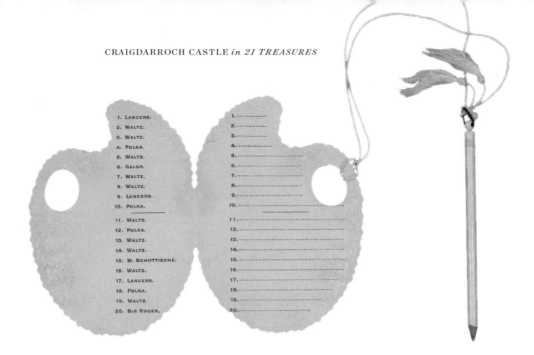

1. LANCERS.	1.
2. WALTZ.	2.
3. WALTZ.	3.
4. POLKA.	4.
5. WALTZ.	5.
6. GALOP.	6.
7. WALTZ.	7.
8. WALTZ.	8.
9. LANCERS.	9.
10. POLKA.	10.
11. WALTZ.	11.
12. POLKA.	12.
13. WALTZ.	13.
14. WALTZ.	14.
15. M. SCHOTTISCHE.	15.
16. WALTZ.	16.
17. LANCERS.	17.
18. POLKA.	18.
19. WALTZ.	19.
20. SIR ROGER.	20.

Each card had a list of the evening's "programme" or dances (polka, waltz, lancers) and their anticipated order, who might be providing the music, and a place for a lady to mark a scheduled partner's name—her "engagements"—or for the partner to pencil himself in.

Sometimes, such as in the pictured example, the dance card had a small pencil attached by a silken cord; sometimes another delicate cord attached it to a lady's wrist.

Dance cards came about in Vienna in the early 1800s, when the fashion had dances become shorter and more numerous, putting ladies at risk of a double booking or a forgotten commitment. Etiquette demanded a lady sit out a dance if she had accidentally double-booked herself.

Judging from the extravagance of the dance card, this 1892 event must have been a big one, yet there was no mention of it in the paper in the days following. Grand balls were often reported on in the society pages. A Victorian ball was a highly ritualized event, and the dance card was a vital part of the ritual.

LADIES NOTED THEIR "ENGAGEMENTS" FOR EACH DANCE WITH THE PENCIL PROVIDED.

20

SUPERINTENDENT
in the PORTE COCHÈRE

HOW COOL: An employee at the Victoria school board just after the Second World War got to go to work in a castle. Victoria College had moved out; additional changes were made and modern conveniences installed to support Craigdarroch Castle's latest function as an educational office building. The frescoed ceiling in the drawing room was painted white (five coats!) and fluorescent lighting was installed. The dining room, which had once held a long baronial dining table and specially made chairs, now contained a very functional table and chairs, so it could be used as a boardroom.

That first year the school board was in residence in the castle (1946), the building was still being heated with coal that had to be shovelled by hand both into the building and into the furnace. Keeping the workplace warm was always a concern, and employees complained about their offices being cold.

School board employees coming to work entered through the double doors on the western side of the building. They then crossed the marble floors of what was originally an entrance designed to provide Joan and her daughters and their guests with exterior egress to the castle's gardens and grounds.

THE OFFICE USED BY THE VICTORIA SCHOOL BOARD ABOVE THE CASTLE'S PORT COCHÈRE.

Employees entered this way because the rounded door currently used was unavailable: the entire porte cochère entrance had been walled in. If you entered the room created for use as the school superintendent's office, the desk where the superintendent sat was framed by a window with a curved top offered by the stone arch on the porte cochère.

The stone and the walls were painted and linoleum placed on the much-trodden floors. It was a utilitarian accommodation with unintended positive consequences: the paint and linoleum protected the original woodwork and walls, making later restoration work easier; the paint that obscured the fresco secco on the drawing room ceiling also shielded it. It ultimately took twelve summers of precise restoration work to return the art piece to its original splendour.

21

TATTING
SHUTTLES

———————————————————

A YOUNG WOMAN born into the moneyed Dunsmuir family—any one of eight daughters or eight granddaughters of the coal baron Robert Dunsmuir and his wife, Joan—is given a decent education (for a girl) thanks, for starters, to the Sisters of St. Ann in Nanaimo. She can read the classics and learn languages and music and how to play billiards—but mostly her job is to make a good marriage. So she learns how to dance and chat and maybe ride, but often she's directed to ladylike activities such as embroidery, knitting, and tatting.

Tatting was a form of fibre art popular in the nineteenth century, reminiscent of the knotted rope work sometimes done by sailors for their sweethearts. Knotting was also used to make thread or yarn or silk cordage appear like floral patterns or beads on a garment. Tatting was used to make a type of lace and edge work for garments, such as collars and cuffs. It was also used to make doilies and antimacassars (for protecting furniture from gentlemen's hair oil). Unlike knitting, which requires a needle in each hand, tatting involves a shuttle held in one hand with the other holding a loop made of the thread or cord being used.

The tatting shuttles in the Craigdarroch collection may well have been used by Joan to show her daughters and granddaughters how it was done. Pretty much all women of that era had some needlework skills—knitting, tatting, crochet, and embroidery—no

Above:

THE MAUCHLINE WARE TATTING
SHUTTLE FROM SCOTLAND

Left:

THE CARVED IVORY TATTING
SHUTTLE FROM CHINA

matter what her status. Tatting lacework was considered a genteel occupation for a gentlewoman. It was popular because it was simple and the supplies easy to obtain.

Thread or cord was wound on the shuttle, which had an elliptical shape. A tail of cord or thread hung free from one end. Loops were formed on the artisan's left hand, and the shuttle was used to feed yarn or cord through the loops to make knots in prescribed patterns, often forming circles with lengths of completed chains of knots before starting a new chain, sometimes with bits of decorative thread or unknotted loops (called picots) hanging free. Sometimes more than one shuttle was used to create designs that were even more complex.

One tatting shuttle in the Craigdarroch collection is made of wood, with the MacLean tartan pattern printed on the surface, and marked "M'Lean" in gold. This piece is about 7.5 centimetres long and is from near a Scottish town called Mauchline in Ayrshire, about twelve kilometres from Hurlford, where Robert Dunsmuir was born. The shuttle dates from the nineteenth century and is believed to be a souvenir item known as "Mauchline ware."

Another is carved ivory and originated in China. It's a bit more compact than the Scottish shuttle, almost 7 centimetres. The carving, on both sides of the implement, shows Chinese figures in domestic and garden scenes.

Collection Creation
A Curator's View

W HEN ASSESSING THE ROLE and the historical importance of Craigdarroch Castle and its collection, people have lots of opinions. There are the history aficionados who love to enter the castle's way-back machine and learn about where parts of Victoria's story were born. There are the tourism promoters who realize what a lure the graceful baronial architecture and the stories of the castle's construction and its inhabitants over the years are. There are the "museum people" who know about the depth and range of the artifacts and documentation both here and at other, similar "house museums" all over North America, the connected string of pearls with the potential ability to explain us to ourselves.

But how better to approach an attempt at understanding than by consulting Bruce Davies, Craigdarroch Castle's curator? He graciously agreed to answer ten of my questions.

BRUCE DAVIES IS CURATOR OF CRAIGDARROCH CASTLE.

How do you see your role as curator at Craigdarroch Castle?
There are a few roles that I have. Some of them are shared by my colleagues. But as the only person at the castle who spent years with [the Castle Society's founder, James K.] Nesbitt, and as one who has done almost every job [at the castle], my perspective is unique. In some ways, I am the institutional memory of the Castle Society.

Participating in all of the decision-making surrounding the conservation of the building's fabric was one of the principal roles that I held for many years ... less so now, [and] that's been a difficult transition for me. That said, I'm part of the team that makes broad-stroke recommendations for treatments to building fabric.

Growing and maintaining the artifact collection has remained a primary role. It's an honour to do it and, conveniently, it's also a lot of fun. I search for and keep tabs on artifacts still in the Dunsmuir family. I also attend auctions and visit antique stores in Victoria and elsewhere.

The objects are used to tell stories, and some objects are associated with many stories. Certain stories are only in my memory, so I'm gradually writing them into the record. The [2020 COVID-19] pandemic has given me time to do this work.

In recent years, many new staff members have joined the society's visitor services department. They are excellent consumers and disseminators of knowledge related to the collection, the building, and the various individuals and institutions who have used it since 1890. One of my roles is to provide them with content in the form of images, textual information, and stories. I help them find what they are looking for. In essence, I am a knowledge facilitator, both in-house and in the wider community.

One of the roles that I see myself having is not actually in my official job description: making money for the castle. It's long been apparent to me—and I think this is something that I learned by observing Mr. Nesbitt—that the longevity and ongoing improvement of the castle is completely dependent on self-generated revenue. I'm always looking at the cost of the things that we do, what value we get from those things, and what initiatives I can support that generate money to further our important work. Government grants, employment programs, and other third-party institutional funding comes and goes. I've watched that happen here for forty-five years. The strength of the Castle Society is that we have never counted on that. Visitation and gift-shop revenue are key.

How did your work with the castle start? How has it changed and grown?

It started by accident—as a summer job. I was hired to be a tour guide while I was in high school. My friend Chris Thom was leaving his castle position and recommended me to Jim Nesbitt. I sat at the front desk and handed out brochures. I gave tours. Whenever Mr. Nesbitt came in, he would send me off to dust the rooms. Sometimes he'd arrive with a car full of stuff that he'd bought at auction or at a local store. I'd bring it into the main hall and then he'd tell me where to hang the pictures and where to place the chairs and tables. It was amazing to me that he knew where everything was. He only went upstairs two or three times per year, but he knew exactly what was on the walls and floor of every room.

When the music conservatory left, I began to do more physical things to the building such as painting and gilding, stripping and refinishing woodwork.

After Mr. Nesbitt died in 1981, there was a prolonged period of organizational upheaval, which really didn't end until 1988. The issues were fairly typical of many organizations—especially non-profit ones. They were about disparate understandings of the mission, competition for power and control—that sort of thing. There were various intertwined factions among board members, volunteers, and staff. Things usually came to a head at the society's annual general meeting and then calmed down for two or three years, and then it would start again. It's wonderful that those days are long gone.

Curiously, a few of these conflicts were about the collection. I remember coming back from Vancouver one day in 1984 with that magnificent Black Forest clock carving [see page 24] in the back of my wife's car. A senior member of the board's furnishings committee, who was a member of an old Victoria family, stopped me in the hallway and asked what it was. I explained that it was a carving that Mrs. Dunsmuir had in the castle when she lived here. "Oh, we don't want that," she insisted. "But it's original to the castle," I said. "Oh no, everybody knew the Dunsmuirs had terrible taste."

I'm still traumatized by that exchange.

Thankfully, those battles are over. Now we have a consistent direction and the place is well resourced. It's very smoothly run, and we have a great board and wonderful senior employees in [Executive Director] John Hughes and [Operations and Development Manager] Giovanni Malcolm.

Operating costs relative to admissions and store revenue have greatly increased in the past fifteen years or so, and this is concerning to me. Concerning not because we're reaching the danger point, but because it is going to take much longer to do the things I want to see done. Historically, we have used operating surpluses to fund capital projects. The annual surpluses are gradually diminishing. This is an unwelcome change from my perspective. I've come to terms with the reality that I likely won't live long enough to see certain things happen.

On the other hand, I've never been denied the money to buy an important object. The castle is also doing some amazing new types of work. The collections database, for example, is a terrific tool used to document artifacts and inform more people than has ever been possible. The degree of training and level of knowledge of our visitor service staff has never been higher. The kitchen/pantry/service area restoration will be a showstopper. The aesthetic experience will be powerful, but unlike [in] the other period rooms in the house, visitors will be allowed to handle things (although they won't be artifacts).

You sometimes talk about the guest experience from a curatorial perspective. Would you tell me about that?

When re-creating a Dunsmuir-era room, like the drawing room or Effie's bedroom, I try to imagine that I am a family member using the space. I consider their interests, personality—even their body size. I move around in the room with differing purposes in mind and think about where they would want to put a certain object, where would this person hang this picture—that sort of thing. Then I put myself in the shoes of the visitor standing at the doorway or behind a security barrier. Sometimes an important artifact won't even be seen by the visitor if I put it where I think it should go to achieve accuracy. In other cases, such as in Maud's bedroom, the place where an artifact should be, like the bed, can't go there because that is where the visitors must stand. So, there is usually a trade-off—adjustments are made.

The drawing room is an interesting case. It's the only room in the castle for which we have photographic evidence from Dunsmuir times. I've used it to guide placement of furniture, paintings, light fixtures, and objets d'art in that room. It clearly shows the Steinway baby grand piano against the north wall. In order to allow visitors to walk through the room, we had to put the piano against the south wall. That said, there is no way of knowing that the Dunsmuirs never placed the piano against the south wall at some point during the eighteen years that they lived there.

We can be sure that when the Dunsmuirs lived in Craigdarroch, they did not have interpretive sign panels and barriers all over the place. They did not welcome 150,000 strangers into their bedrooms each year. The act of making the house accessible to visitors necessarily diminishes the authenticity of the place. Striking a balance is an ongoing challenge. The ideal balance is subjective and there is never 100 percent agreement among those involved in operating the museum.

What are the biggest challenges facing a living museum such as Craigdarroch? Too many visitors with consequent asset wear and tear? Not enough visitors?
Without a doubt, there is a correlation between the number of visitors in the building at any one time and the quality of a visitor's experience.

There is a visceral draw to Craigdarroch for most people. It's just a house—granted, not a normal house, but it's a house nonetheless, and everyone gets that. Then there is the voyeuristic intrigue of seeing someone else's very special house. If you asked most visitors whether they would like to tour the castle alone, or with their limited group while no one else was in the place, I think that most people would say "Yes." And if you could let them do that without interpretive signs and barriers, well, that would easily be the most authentic-feeling experience imaginable.

Some people feel that the castle is boring and lifeless without myriad interpretive aids. I'm not one of them. It just takes imagination, and I believe that everyone has that.

The conservation of the building and the care of its museum collection is extremely expensive. Craigdarroch's visitors pay for this important work through their admission fees and museum store purchases. And so, we need to have visitors, and if we did not have visitors, what would be the point of doing what we do here?

Too many visitors causes harm to the building. They rub the walls and artifacts with their packs, scratch doors and other surfaces, and deposit enormous amounts of dust and small pebbles throughout the building. This happens even after they are subjected to our carefully implemented entrance procedures. On the plus side, the more we do to restore the place, the better it gets, and with time, the rarer it becomes. Consequently, experiencing it becomes more valuable. We can charge more money to come in, and to some degree, we can limit numbers that way. But we must ensure that students and underprivileged people are not excluded because of cost, and I think this has been successfully navigated by the Castle Society from the beginning.

When I started here in 1975, there was no admission charge. Everyone came in and left through the Garden Entrance. More than half of the house wasn't even officially open to the public because the music conservatory was here. Despite that, we had annual visitation of about 115,000–120,000 [people]. . . . Mr. Nesbitt calculated that, on average, we received a twenty-five-cent donation from each visitor. That model was unsustainable, but resistance to implementation of an admission charge in the 1980s was formidable.

In the world of museums in the twenty-first century, do you think there is too much focus on transition to digital delivery and not enough on collection growth and maintenance?
I can't really speak to this precisely because I don't know enough about what is going on in the rest of the world. . . . That said, I feel that the digital experience within a museum/gallery building can greatly detract from interaction with artifacts. All over the world, I've seen museum visitors struggling with devices or focusing primarily on the content they are providing, while seemingly not even seeing the thing(s) the technology is supposed to explain.

I think technological intrusion into historic interiors is especially problematic. In the context of a house museum, it can easily become just one more visual and audio intrusion into a place that is supposed to feel and look like someone's home 130 years ago. There are ways to mitigate this tendency through good design, but it's not easy, and it is most certainly expensive. A museum should not try to appeal to every type of visitor conceivable if it causes something more important to be left undone.

Technology performs a great service to the museum visitor who can't physically enter the museum to see or hear the collection—for whatever reason.

What are your thoughts on asset acquisition (and reacquisition!) versus re-creation?

I fall on the acquisition or reacquisition side.

For me, reproductions (and excessive signage) tend to make museums into large three-dimensional picture books. It is the magic of the real object that enthralls and inspires.

If an object is original to Craigdarroch but can't be obtained or displayed, then I'm very much in favour of making a reproduction of it and displaying that.

What do you think we in the here and now have to learn from the way people lived in the Victorian era? During other eras, and from other subcultures, represented by the castle's collections?

Today's health care is marvellous. Medical treatment for diseases like breast cancer in the Victorian era would be considered barbaric by today's standards. I suspect that people one hundred years from now will look back at us today and think the same thing.

Many objects in our collection—the needlework items, the books, the paintings, the musical instruments, etc.—show us that in the past, people devoted more time than we do today to reading paper books, making things with their hands, and to a variety of artistic pursuits.

What do you think is the gift, in both the short and longer term, of Craigdarroch Castle and its collection to Victoria? To BC? To Canada and Canadians?

I feel the castle building and the domestic material inside it as being one entity—a place of beauty and a window to another era. In that sense, it has universal meaning to all people, regardless of when and where they live in the world. To the citizens of Greater Victoria, ease of physical access to such a place is a significant gift. Naturally, ease of access diminishes the farther one lives from it, but Craigdarroch's fabric and its associated stories are becoming increasingly accessible to those who can't visit.

An often-overlooked gift the castle brings locally, regionally, and nationally is economic. The building is the most visited historic site in the province and probably in western Canada, with 130,000–160,000 annual visits. Many of these visitors stay in hotels, eat in restaurants, take taxis, buy gifts, etc. Service providers, our employees and contractors gain employment, and all levels of government receive tax revenue. This is a scenario that has been at least partially playing out since the 1890s when Mrs. Dunsmuir was living here.

What would you most like to see Craigdarroch do next in terms of the building? The collection? Programming? The visitor experience? Inside the castle, I'd like to see the kitchen, butler's pantry, and the related service areas finished. This will be a visual and experiential treat for visitors. We envision a hands-on presentation where people can touch the objects (they won't be artifacts in the collection per se) and interact with our staff and docents. Perhaps our visitors will even cook some things!

Next, I would like to see the guest bedroom on the second floor finished. This is the room directly above the dining room. It is the room where Alexander Dunsmuir stayed when visiting from San Francisco. It is where his discussions with his brother, James, about his will took place. It's documented in court testimony. In some ways it is the epicentre, the main story of the Dunsmuir family—the wrenching asunder of a great family in the quest for money and power. From an aesthetic and presentation standpoint, I can see exactly what the room will look like. This room will be a showstopper. It would undoubtedly be the most important nineteenth-century bedroom presentation in Canada. I want to do it before I retire.

Next, I would like to see the installation of the galleries planned for Mrs. Dunsmuir's bedroom and in the second bedroom (a.k.a. Jessie's bedroom). These galleries will enable us to bring out of storage and/or more effectively display a wide range of artifacts in our collection that have direct connections to Dunsmuir family members. We have some extraordinary artifacts that visitors know nothing about.

There are a few things that I'd most like to see happen [to the] outside of the castle.

First is the completion of the current . . . work involving stone conservation and rainwater downpipe treatments. Next, I'd like to see some resolution to the matter of the finial on the top of the tower. There is currently a copper cone there. Originally there was a rather elaborate and tall weather vane, but it was bent in a storm soon after it was installed in 1889. Years later, Mrs. Dunsmuir replaced it with a nicely shaped copper finial, which we have in storage. The decision must be made whether to put that copper finial back or install a wind-resistant weather vane similar to the original one. . . . Next, I'd like to see the above-ground floodlight fixtures replaced by underground fixtures or by fixtures mounted on the roofs of neighbouring buildings owned by the Castle Society. . . . Planting vegetation around the south and west sides of the castle using historic Dunsmuir-era photographs as guides for types and placement would enhance the aesthetic qualities and accuracy of site presentation.

Is there anything you'd like me to know about Craigdarroch's collection and your curatorial work that hasn't been elicited by my questions?

Issues surrounding preventive conservation of collections in house museums, and historic buildings, through environmental controls [are] unique and challenging. Improper relative humidity, ultraviolet and visible light levels, and temperature extremes can contribute to shortening the lifespan of all artifacts. Paper and textiles are especially susceptible to light damage. Wood too, but it is a little less sensitive. Metal likes dry conditions. Stone is the least sensitive. Nothing likes too much or too little relative humidity. Artifacts in house museums are often made of combinations of materials, with each material having unique environmental needs. That is a problem. In the museum world, it is often called "inherent vice."

Another problem is that the house museum building is itself an artifact that must be preserved. Attempts made to mechanically control environmental conditions in the house can be disastrous. . . .

At Craigdarroch, we respect the way the building has coexisted with the outside environment during the past 130 years. We heat the building in the winter, and while it is often too dry for collections, it's not as bad as it would be if the castle was in, say, Chicago or Edmonton. If we kept the building interior at a temperature ideal for collections during winter, which would probably be about six degrees Celsius, we'd have some unhappy visitors and staff! I'm thinking back a few years to a winter when we had no operating boiler for about three months. The artifacts loved that, but no one else did.

[Earlier tenants] destroyed most of the original wooden window shutters [that] the Dunsmuirs used to control visible light in the rooms. We've been gradually installing reproductions of these shutters to great effect. They reduce light levels and also increase the authenticity of the rooms and the castle's exterior appearance.

Another issue surrounding light levels is visitor experience. Without the window shutters, a lot of light comes into the rooms through the windows. People look at the windows, especially the stained glass, and this constricts the pupils of their eyes. Then they look at a picture in the corner of the room and conclude that the room is too dark to see the artifact when in fact it is not. They just need to stop looking at the window so that their pupils dilate. In other cases, a given area is actually too dark for optimal viewing, but the light level is historically accurate.

The collection is evolving. With the exception of Effie's bedroom, none of the period rooms at Craigdarroch is finished.

IMAGE CREDITS

*Craigdarroch Castle Collection
refers to the castle's archive,
Craigdarroch Castle photos
to images that appear courtesy
of castle staff.

BIBLIOGRAPHY

Bowen, Lynne. *Robert Dunsmuir: Laird of the Mines*. Montreal: XYZ Publishing, 1999.

Bridge, Kathryn. *Henry & Self: An English Gentlewoman at the Edge of Empire*. Victoria, BC: Royal BC Museum, 2019.

Chamberlain, Paul. *Victoria's Castles: A Brief History of Lovers, Madmen, Millionaires, and Ghosts on Canada's Imperial Margins*. Victoria, BC: Dingle House Press, 2012.

Craigdarroch Castle Historical Museum Society. *Craigdarroch Castle: Canada's Castle*. Victoria, BC: Craigdarroch Castle Historical Museum Society, 2014.

Davies, Bruce. *Craigdarroch Military Hospital: A Canadian War Story*. Victoria, BC: Craigdarroch Castle Historical Museum Society, 2019.

Green, Valerie. *Above Stairs: Social Life in Upper-Class Victoria 1843–1918*. Victoria, BC: Sono Nis Press, 1995.

Reksten, Terry. *Craigdarroch: The Story of Dunsmuir Castle*. Victoria, BC: Orca Book Publishers, 1987.

Reksten, Terry. *The Dunsmuir Saga*. Vancouver, BC: Douglas & McIntyre, 1991.

Reksten, Terry. *More English Than the English: A Very Social History of Victoria*. Victoria, BC: Sono Nis Press, 2011.

INDEX

ABOUT THE AUTHOR

Sam Bufalini

MOIRA DANN is a writer, editor, speaker, and current president of the Craigdarroch Castle Museum Society board. She has a Master of Fine Arts in creative non-fiction from the University of King's College and is a former editor of the *Globe & Mail*'s Facts and Arguments page. She lives with her husband, Sam Bufalini, in Victoria, BC.